# TECHNICAL ANALYSIS FOR THE REST OF US

# TECHNICAL ANALYSIS FOR THE REST OF US

What Every Investor Needs to Know to Increase Income, Minimize Risk, and Achieve Capital Gains

**CLIFFORD PISTOLESE**

**McGraw-Hill**

New York   Chicago   San Francisco
Lisbon   London   Madrid   Mexico City
Milan   New Delhi   San Juan   Seoul
Singapore   Sydney   Toronto

*The **McGraw·Hill** Companies*

3 4 5 6 7 8 9 0    FGR / FGR    0 9 8

ISBN 0-07-146721-1

This publication is designed to provide accurate and authoritative information in regard to the subject matter covered. It is sold with the understanding that neither the author nor the publisher is engaged in rendering legal, accounting, futures/securities trading, or other professional service. If legal advice or other expert assistance is required, the services of a competent professional person should be sought.

*—From a Declaration of Principles jointly adopted by a Committee of the American Bar Association and a Committee of Publishers*

McGraw-Hill books are available at special quantity discounts to use as premiums and sales promotions, or for use in corporate training programs. For more information, please write to the Director of Special Sales, Professional Publishing, McGraw-Hill, Two Penn Plaza, New York, NY 10121-2298. Or contact your local bookstore.

I dedicate this book to my wife, Ramona. She has Alzheimer's Disease and is in a nursing home. She can no longer talk or understand speech, but we still communicate with smiles, gentle touches, and eye contact. I am with her for a few hours every day and know our love will continue until death parts us.

# CONTENTS

# PREFACE

Technical analysis has become a very popular method for understanding and profiting from what is happening in the stock market. One reason for its popularity is that it has shown its usefulness through the bull and bear markets of past decades. Another reason is that it is based on the fundamental relationship between supply and demand and explains how these two opposed forces interact to provide clues to the direction of stock prices. The third and most important reason for its popularity is that investors who develop skill in using technical analysis learn how to buy near price bottoms and sell near tops.

Financial programs on television show many charts that contain stock price patterns. After studying the contents of this book, you will be able to interpret a stock price pattern and come to your own conclusion about the prospects for a stock. This is advantageous because some of the guests on television programs are not skilled at technical analysis and offer erroneous interpretations of price patterns.

Here is an outline of the content of this book. Chapters 1 through 3 present information on how to analyze stock price patterns, volume of trading data, and moving averages of stock prices. These three subject areas form the basis of technical analysis as it is applied to individual stocks. The last six chapters provide guidance in the broader context of how to apply technical analysis to a variety of investment activities and opportunities as follows:

Chapter 4 describes three types of portfolios—aggressive, balanced, and conservative and gives guidelines for choosing the most suitable one for the various phases of the market.

Chapter 5 explains the three basic approaches to the market—active short-term trading, making intermediate-term transactions, and investing for the long term.

Chapter 6 describes the best Web sites on the Internet that provide free stock price charts and a wide variety of data and technical indicators helpful to technical analysts.

Chapter 7 describes the benefits of closed-end funds and explains their advantages over traditional mutual funds.

Chapter 8 focuses on preferred stocks and illustrates how they can be bought both for high dividends and capital gains.

Chapter 9 outlines the basics of real estate investment trusts (REITs) and indicates how they can be a good source of high dividends.

If you have been dependent on the recommendations of a stock broker to make purchases and sales, you can now develop the ability to make decisions more independently. This is an important benefit because sometimes a broker's advice serves his or her interest more than yours.

Using technical analysis effectively is a skill, and the acquisition of a skill requires practice. You will have many opportunities to practice interpreting stock price patterns, moving averages, and trading volume data. Conscientious participation in these exercises is the most important part of this learning process. With a studious attitude, you can develop an enlightened approach to the market and enjoy the rewards of investing successfully.

# TECHNICAL ANALYSIS FOR THE REST OF US

# 1

# BASIC CONCEPTS OF TECHNICAL ANALYSIS

## INTRODUCTION

As an investor in the stock market, you are faced with the challenge of choosing from among thousands of potential investments. To be successful in this effort you need a method for distinguishing desirable, timely investments from those that are undesirable or untimely. Technical analysis is a methodology by which this distinction can be made.

It's not possible for you to know everything that affects the financial fortunes of a company. However, all that is known about a company's prospects is reflected in a stock price chart that summarizes the results of all the transactions in its stock.

## SUPPLY AND DEMAND

If buyers are more eager to buy than sellers are to sell, the demand for a stock is greater than the supply, and the price goes up. If sellers are more eager to sell than buyers are to buy, the supply of a stock is more than the demand, and the price goes down. The eagerness of buyers and sellers is usually unequal, which produces the price fluctuations and patterns visible in stock price charts. A

technical analyst observes this pictorial representation of the contest between the buyers and sellers and looks for clues as to which
side is likely to win. This chapter will help you get started in the
hunt for, and interpretation of, these clues.

Technical analysis provides a comprehensive and valuable
source of information on which to base decisions. This is why many
professionals in the financial world use technical analysis to make
investments on behalf of their clients and for their own accounts.
As public awareness of technical analysis grows by way of articles
in newspapers and magazines and by presentations by technical
analysts on financial television programs, many investors have
begun using this method to make their own investment decisions.
After reading this book, you will be able to develop your own
capacity to evaluate stocks and make profitable investments in the
market.

Note that the chart patterns you will see are idealized for
instructional purposes. Identifying actual price patterns may be
difficult at first, but through practice and experience, you can
become skilled in this art. In the sections that follow, you will learn
to recognize the price patterns that form the basis for the practice of
technical analysis.

## UPWARD PRICE TREND

Refer to Chart 1-1. An *upward price trend* is defined by a series of
ascending short-term bottoms. These rising bottoms indicate that
buyers are more eager to buy than sellers are to sell. An uptrend is
established tentatively when the second bottom is higher than the
first. The uptrend is confirmed when the third bottom is higher
than the second. Uptrends that rise at angles between 10 and 30
degrees are sustainable for a long time and can produce large capital gains. Uptrends that rise at rates between 30 and 50 degrees
are less sustainable, but can generate high profits in intermediate
time periods. Uptrends that rise at a faster rate than 50 degrees are

**CHART 1-1**

Upward Price Trend

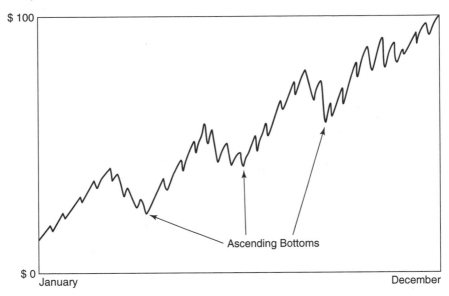

$100

$0

January                                                      December

Ascending Bottoms

short lived, but can produce very high profits. Unfortunately, this type of fast rise in price is often followed by an equally fast decline.

## DOWNWARD PRICE TREND

Refer to Chart 1-2. A *downward price trend* is defined by a series of descending short-term tops. When the second top is lower than the first top, a downtrend is established tentatively. When the third top is lower than the second top, the downtrend is confirmed. A downtrend indicates sellers are more eager to sell than buyers are to buy. Some investors see a stock price falling and decide it is a bargain at some level. Unfortunately, there is no way to predict where a downtrend will end. Buying a stock in a downtrend is usually a losing endeavor.

**CHART 1-2**

Downward Price Trend

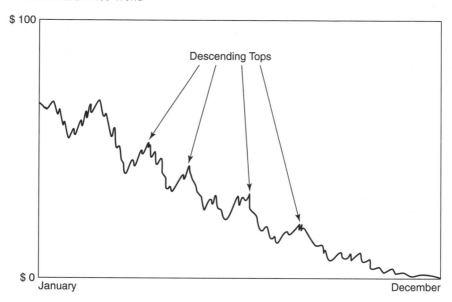

## TRADING RANGE

Refer to Chart 1-3. A *trading range* is a series of price fluctuations within a delineated vertical distance. Each trading range has its own limits, which can be narrow, wide, or anywhere in between. The top of a trading range is a *resistance level,* the price at which holders of the stock are eager to sell. The bottom of a trading range is a *support level,* the price at which investors are eager to buy. The life span of a trading range can be as short as a week or two or can last for months. A long-lasting trading range presents many opportunities for profitable transactions. An experienced trader takes advantage of the situation by buying near the support level and selling near the resistance level. The risk is that the price will eventually break out to the upside or the downside. If a trader has just bought near the support level and the price of the stock breaks out to the downside, the trader is faced with a potential loss. If a trader has just sold near the resistance level and the

CHART 1-3

Trading Range

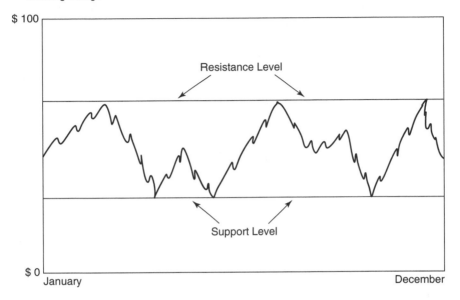

stock breaks out to the upside, the trader has missed an opportunity for a larger gain. Many traders take those risks in the hope that their profits gained from trading within the range will more than compensate for any subsequent losing transaction or missed opportunity.

## HEAD AND SHOULDERS

Refer to Chart 1-4. A *head and shoulders* pattern can develop at the end of a long rise where the stock has become very overpriced. This pattern is a warning that the price is probably going to drop to much lower levels. The longer the pattern takes to form, and the larger the pattern is in terms of height, the further the price will probably decline. If you are holding a stock that has formed a head and shoulders pattern, sell it after a downtrend from the top of the right shoulder has been confirmed.

**C H A R T   1-4**

Head and Shoulders

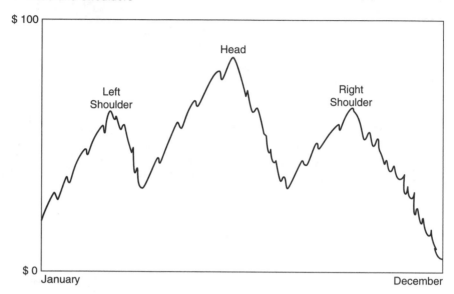

Chart 1-4 presents an idealized representation. Some head and shoulders patterns will not be as symmetrical because one shoulder may be higher or lower than the other, and some will have more than one shoulder on one side or on both sides. But so long as the head has at least one shoulder on each side, the pattern is valid.

## DOUBLE TOP

Refer to Chart 1-5. *Double tops* develop because stockholders who didn't sell at the first top don't want to miss that opportunity the second time the price rises to that high level. Double tops can form in a few weeks or months, or in longer than a year. The price decline from a double top will probably be extensive no matter how far the distance between the tops. Preserve your capital and don't buy a stock after a double top forms; if you own it, sell it after a down-trend has been established and confirmed from the second top.

**CHART 1-5**

Double Top

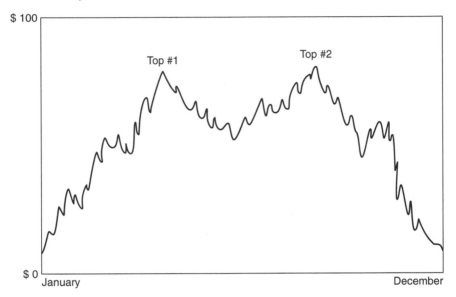

In some cases, the second top will be slightly above or below the first top. And on rare occasions, a third top will develop. Whatever the configuration, the price of the stock is very likely to go much lower.

## ROUNDING TOP

Refer to Chart 1-6. A *rounding top* is a formation that gradually converts an uptrend into a downtrend. The center of the rounding top is called the *distribution phase*. This is a period when well-informed investors realize the stock is very overpriced and they sell (distribute) their holdings to less knowledgeable investors. As the demand for the stock lessens, the price starts to decline gradually and a downtrend develops. The establishment and confirmation of the downtrend is the signal to sell. This price formation has the shape of an upside-down saucer. Some rounding tops do not follow such

**CHART 1-6**

Rounding Top

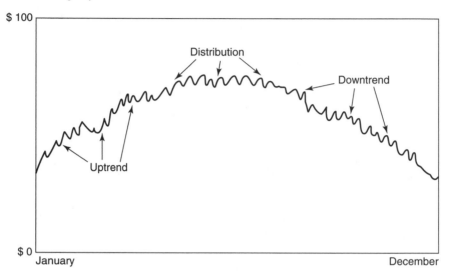

a smooth, gentle curve. They may have jagged areas, large bumps, or other irregular features.

## SYMMETRICAL TRIANGLE

Refer to Chart 1-7. A *symmetrical triangle* forms when the stockholders who want to sell and buyers who want to buy the stock are equally eager. A downtrend forms the upper side of the triangle as the stockholders sell at lower and lower prices. And an uptrend forms the bottom side of the triangle as buyers are willing to pay higher and higher prices. Most of the time a breakout occurs before the apex of the triangle is reached. But if the price exits through the apex in a horizontal direction, the triangle loses its relevance. After an upside or downside breakout, the price usually rises or falls a distance at least equal to the height of the triangle.

Note that it only takes two tops and two bottoms to establish the top and bottom trendlines of the triangle. This is a large trian-

CHART 1-7

Symmetrical Triangle

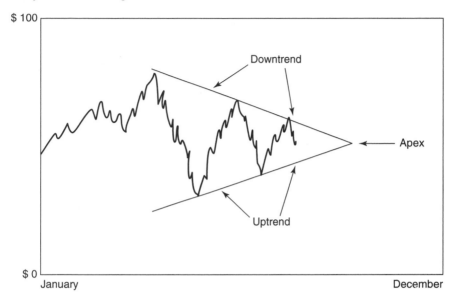

gle, as indicated by its height of about $50 as measured from the first top within the triangle to the trendline directly below it.

## ASCENDING TRIANGLE

Refer to Chart 1-8. An *ascending triangle* is an unequal contest, with buyers being more eager than sellers. For a while the sellers are convinced a particular price is a good place to sell, and this deter-mination creates a horizontal line as the resistance level. During that period, the buyers become more eager and are willing to pay higher and higher prices, which creates the uptrend line as the lower side of the triangle.

The breakout is almost always to the upside, and the price continues in that direction. The initial size of the price rise will probably be a distance about equal to the height of the triangle. If the price goes out through the apex, the triangle has no further

**CHART 1-8**

Ascending Triangle

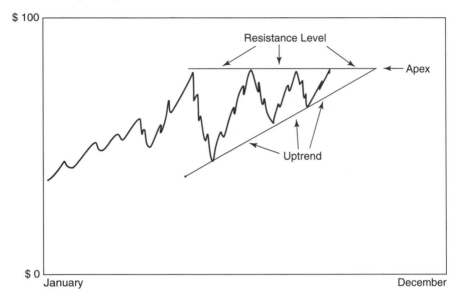

price implication. On rare occasions, the breakout will be to the downside, so it is best to wait and buy only if the price goes up through the resistance level.

## DESCENDING TRIANGLE

Refer to Chart 1-9. A *descending triangle* is an unequal contest, with the sellers being more eager than the buyers. For a while the buyers are convinced a particular price is a bargain, and they buy enough to create a support level at that price. However, since the sellers are more eager than the buyers, they are willing to accept lower and lower prices, and usually the price breaks out to the downside. If the price goes out through the apex, the contest has ended in a stalemate and the triangle becomes irrelevant. On rare occasions, the price breaks out to the upside, so holders of the stock should wait for a breakout before deciding what to do.

**CHART 1-9**

Descending Triangle

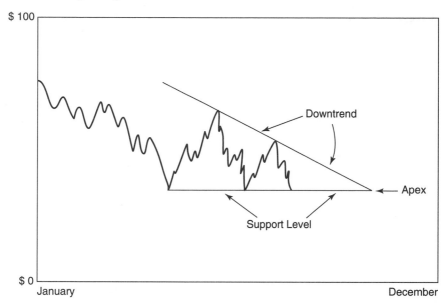

## INVERTED HEAD AND SHOULDERS

Refer to Chart 1-10. An *inverted head and shoulders* pattern develops after a long drop in price. This pattern implies the stock is very underpriced and is probably going to rise to higher levels. This formation usually takes a few months to form. Either shoulder may be lower or higher than the other, and there may be more than one shoulder on either side. Inverted head and shoulders patterns provide an opportunity for a large capital gain. The time to buy is after an uptrend has been established and confirmed as the price rises from the bottom of the second shoulder.

## ROUNDING BOTTOM

Refer to Chart 1-11. A *rounding bottom* is a formation that gradually converts a downtrend into an uptrend. The bottom part of the formation is called the *accumulation phase*. This is a period when the

## CHART 1-10

### Inverted Head and Shoulders

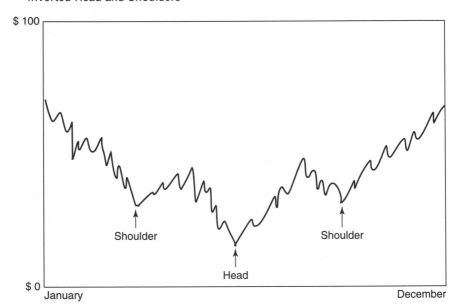

## CHART 1-11

### Rounding Bottom

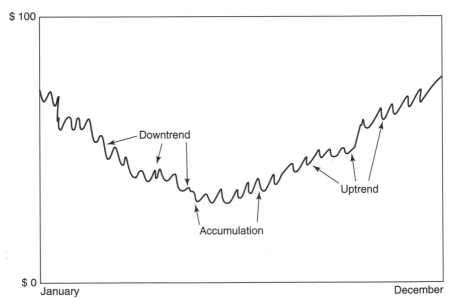

most knowledgeable investors believe the stock is very undervalued and buy all that's offered. As the supply of stock gradually diminishes, the price momentum shifts to the upside and the price starts to rise. This formation represents an excellent opportunity for a large capital gain. The time to buy is after an uptrend has been established and confirmed.

## DOUBLE BOTTOM

Refer to Chart 1-12. *Double bottoms* develop because investors who didn't buy at the first bottom don't want to miss the opportunity to buy at the lowest level again. Double bottoms can form in a few weeks, months, or longer than a year. The rise in price is usually large, no matter how long between the two bottoms. The time to buy is after an uptrend has been established and confirmed from the second bottom.

### CHART 1-12

Double Bottom

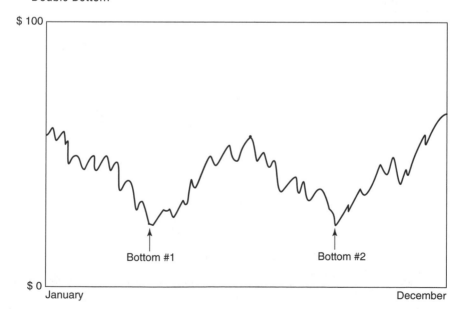

## CHART 1-13

Parabolic Curve

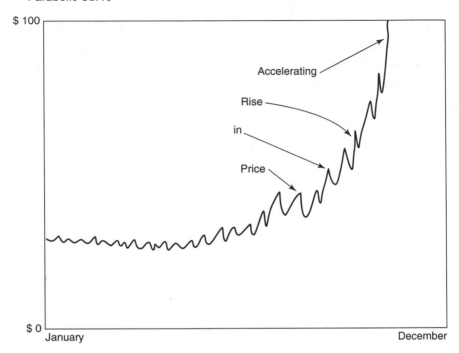

$ 100

Accelerating

Rise

in

Price

$ 0
January                                                    December

## CHART 1-14

Flat Line

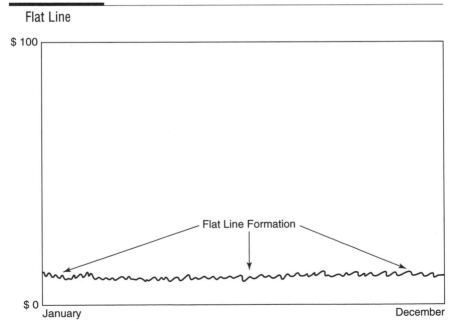

$ 100

Flat Line Formation

$ 0
January                                                    December

## PARABOLIC CURVE

Refer to Chart 1-13. The *parabolic curve* is an impressive type of curve that illustrates a stock price that accelerates until it is going almost straight up. This sky-rocketing price indicates excessive speculation. An investor should be wary of buying in this type of situation. At some point that is impossible to predict, no more buyers want to speculate on further price advances and the final result (not shown here) is likely to be a steep and extended price decline.

**CHART 1-15**

Erratic Price Volatility

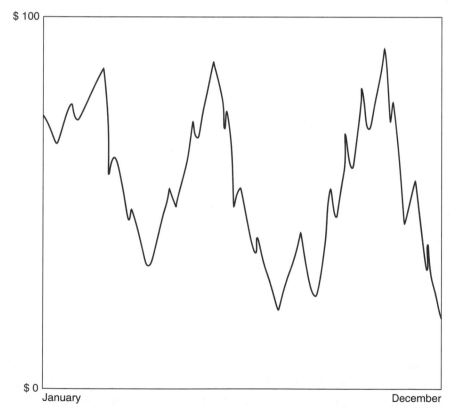

January                                        December

## FLAT LINE FORMATION

Refer to Chart 1-14. A *flat line formation* indicates there is extremely little buying or selling interest in a stock. Both the sellers and the buyers are in agreement that the very low price is justified. Buying a stock with this type of line formation is usually a waste of time. Let this one stay in its dormant condition and look for other more promising prospects.

## ERRATIC VOLATILITY

Refer to Chart 1-15. Exceptionally volatile stocks are not amenable to pattern analysis because their fluctuations are random and do not form any recognizable patterns. These stocks are very risky because their price movements are so difficult to predict. It's best not to try to guess what the price will do next.

## MATCH-UP EXERCISE

Chart 1-16 presents an exercise you can use to check how well you have learned the information presented in this chapter. Fifteen price patterns are shown.

Also shown are the names of the various patterns. Match the name of each pattern to the pattern itself and write the number of the pattern inside the box showing the pattern. When you are finished, check your answers against those presented in Chart 1-17.

## A NOTE OF CAUTION

Investing in stocks on the basis of analyzing stock price patterns should improve your ability to select winners and avoid losers. However, using technical analysis cannot eliminate the inherent risks in the stock market. Consequently, when buying the stock of any individual company, no matter how well respected, it's best to limit the amount of money you invest to a small percentage of your total assets.

## CHART 1-16

Match-Up Exercise

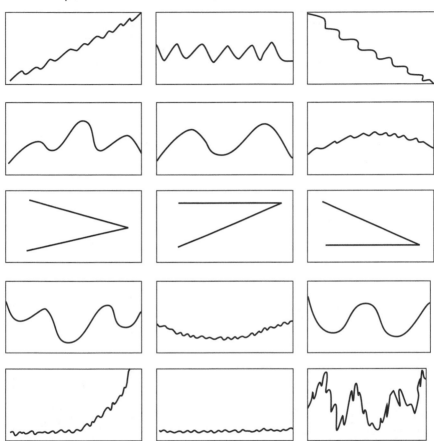

1. Ascending Triangle
2. Double Bottom
3. Flat Line Formation
4. Descending Triangle
5. Rounding Bottom
6. Parabolic Curve
7. Inverted Head and Shoulders

8. Uptrend
9. Head and Shoulders
10. Trading Range
11. Downtrend
12. Double Top
13. Symmetrical Triangle
14. Rounding Top
15. Erratic Volatility

## CHART 1-17

### Match-Up Exercise (Answers)

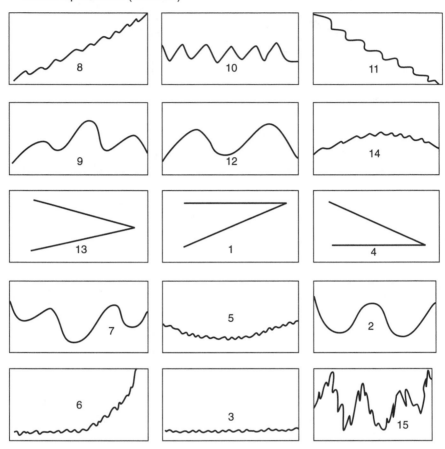

1. Ascending Triangle
2. Double Bottom
3. Flat Line Formation
4. Descending Triangle
5. Rounding Bottom
6. Parabolic Curve
7. Inverted Head and Shoulders

8. Uptrend
9. Head and Shoulders
10. Trading Range
11. Downtrend
12. Double Top
13. Symmetrical Triangle
14. Rounding Top
15. Erratic Volatility

# 2

# VOLUME ANALYSIS

## INTRODUCTION

Some investors check the prices of their stocks every day, but don't look at the trading volume. Those investors are uninformed about a major factor affecting the prospects for their stocks. Staying aware of how many shares are traded in a stock helps an investor estimate the level of significance in price movements.

If a stock makes an unexpected move to the upside and there's no news on the company, a large increase in trading volume indicates something significant has probably happened, but has not yet been reported. This price movement prior to a news report is a common occurrence because information about a major event within a company is often leaked before the official news release is published.

On the other hand, a price move with a small or no increase in trading volume is more likely to develop from a temporary imbalance in the supply and demand relationship. Watching the volume of trading and making comparisons to average trading volume enables an investor to distinguish between price moves that can develop momentum and those that are just meaningless random movements.

The main point to remember is that a large increase in volume validates a price move to the upside, while a small or no increase in trading volume discredits it. To be well informed and have an objective basis for making investment decisions, an investor should monitor the relationship between price moves and trading volume.

## AVERAGE VOLUME DATA

It's important to know what the average trading volume is for a stock you may want to buy or which you are holding. This gives you a way to judge the significance of price movements by comparing the current trading volume against the average volume. If the average trading volume is hundreds of thousands of shares per day, an increase to millions of shares daily as the stock price moves higher indicates something positive has happened with regard to the company. Data on average trading volume is available on www.Yahoo.Finance.com and other financial Web sites.

## TRADING VOLUME AND THE STOCK MARKET

Checking the total trading volume can also provide a clue as to whether the stock market will rise or fall. If the stock market averages rise and the volume of trading increases, it's an indication the market is likely to go higher. If the averages rise, but the volume of trading stays flat or declines, it indicates the market is unlikely to go up much further.

Another factor in the analysis is the length of time a relationship between price movement and volume of trading lasts. A one- or two-day rise in the market averages with higher trading volume has short-term significance. A one- or two-week rise in the averages with a large increase in the volume of trading means the averages are likely to rise for an intermediate period of time. And a coincident rise in the market averages and the trading volume for around a month can set the stage for a long-term rise.

## STOCK PRICE AND TRADING VOLUME CHARTS

Every chart in this chapter has an additional section that shows how the volume of trading relates to stock price fluctuations.

Reviewing these charts and the associated comments will help you to see how trading volume affects the strength and durability of an early-stage stock price move. Each chart shows a relationship between the price pattern, a breakout from the pattern, and the trading volume. With each chart is an explanation of these relationships.

Refer to Chart 2-1. After failing several times to break out above the resistance level, the stock price finally starts moving up with a large increase in trading volume both before and after the breakout. This implies the price rise will continue a while. The increase in trading volume at the breakout means many additional investors have become buyers of the stock because they believe a

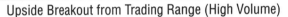

**CHART 2-1**

Upside Breakout from Trading Range (High Volume)

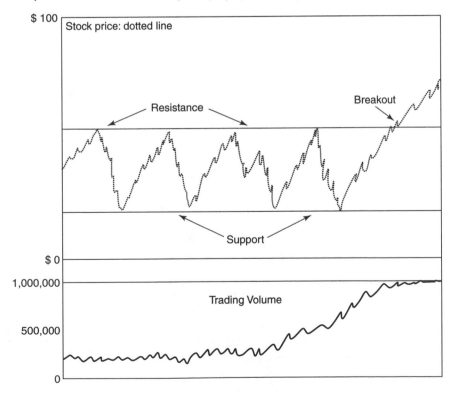

significant improvement in the prospects for the company has occurred.

Refer to Chart 2-2. Note that the trading volume during the period before and after the breakout has only increased slightly above the average trading volume of the preceding time period. Few new investors are investing at this time. This breakout may be only a temporary imbalance in the relationship between supply and demand. The stock price may stay above the breakout point for some time, but the small increase in volume indicates the price is unlikely to go much higher.

Refer to Chart 2-3. This chart shows a false breakout from a trading range. Fortunately, these are rare. An investor not paying

## CHART 2-2

Upside Breakout from Trading Range (Low Volume)

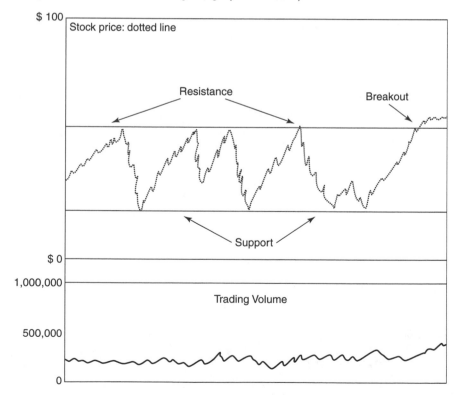

## CHART 2-3

False Breakout from Trading Range

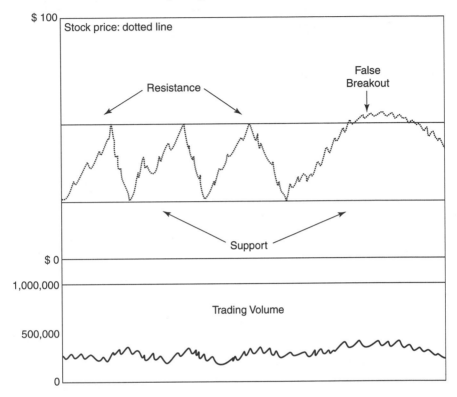

attention to the day's volume of trading and noticing the initial price breakout might think this is a good opportunity to buy, but it could be a trap. It is a matter of conjecture as to why low-volume breakouts occur. Perhaps a positive rumor was circulated about this company and the price rose temporarily. When the rumor proved to be false, the price reverted to its previous location within the trading range. By noting the low level of volume at the breakout and afterwards, an alert investor can avoid being lured into an unrewarding situation.

Refer to Chart 2-4. Here you see a price break out to the downside on a large increase in volume. This increase could be caused by some problem within the company. Probably those stockholders

**CHART 2-4**

Downside Breakout from Trading Range

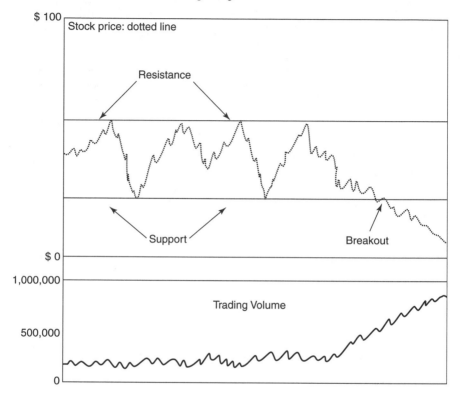

who have become aware of the situation have sold, and others have followed their lead. Having broken through the support level on an increase in volume, the stock price is likely to drop fast and the extent of the fall is probably going to be large.

Refer to Chart 2-5. This is the type of symmetrical triangle that develops when both buyers and sellers are becoming eager. The buyers are willing to pay higher prices as time passes, and the sellers are eager to sell for lower prices. Gradually the balance between supply and demand changes in favor of the buyers, who want more shares than are available at these price levels. In this situation, the extra demand forces a breakout to the upside.

## CHART 2-5

Upside Breakout from Symmetrical Triangle

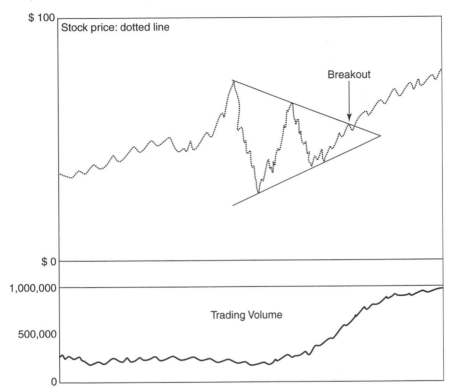

The large rise in trading volume was a leading indication that the price would break out to the upside. Note that the high trading volume is continuing as the price moves above the highest point in the triangle. This is a sign the price will rise for a while.

Refer to Chart 2-6. This chart demonstrates the exception to the rule that an increase in trading volume is required for a price movement to be large. A significant move to the upside must be supported by an increase in volume. But a price move to the down-side can be large when there is little or no increase in trading volume. All it takes for a stock price to move down is a lack of demand on the part of the buyers. Without this support, a stock

## CHART 2-6

Downside Breakout from Symmetrical Triangle

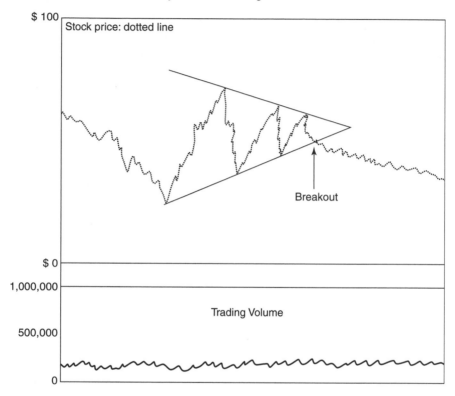

price can drift lower over time and the price drop can be sizeable. The breakout to the downside might be caused by a minor problem that results in some potential buyers withdrawing their bids. Whatever the reason, buyers have lost interest in this stock and until something revives their enthusiasm, the price will probably drift lower.

Refer to Chart 2-7. Ascending triangles provide a visual representation of rising demand absorbing a limited supply. Because of this unbalanced relationship, when an ascending triangle forms, the implication is that the breakout will be to the upside. In this case, the large increase in trading volume that occurred along with the breakout indicates the price will continue rising for a while. The

## CHART 2-7

Upside Breakout from Ascending Triangle

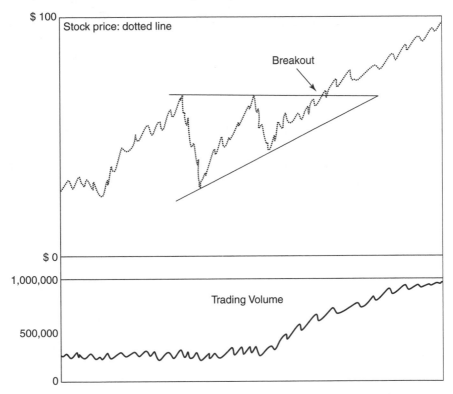

minimum expectation is that the rise in price will be equal to the height of the triangle.

Refer to Chart 2-8. This descending triangle represents an unequal contest between sellers who are more eager to sell than buyers are to buy. The expected result is realized when the price breaks out to the downside. The large increase in trading volume during the breakout validates the price move. Once the breakout has happened, the probability is that the decline will persist for a while longer unless something happens to improve the prospects for the company. If the breakout had occurred with little or no increase in trading volume, the subsequent decline would probably be slower, but could go just as far.

## CHART 2-8

Downside Breakout from Descending Triangle

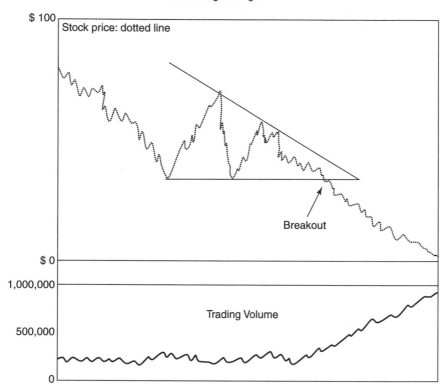

Refer to Chart 2-9. After the breakout from the downtrend occurred, an uptrend was established. The trading volume increased and continued as the price rose. It's impossible to know when a downtrend will end or whether an uptrend will follow. This means it's best to buy only after a breakout rather than try to guess when the downtrend will stop.

Refer to Chart 2-10. After the breakout from this uptrend a downtrend was established. The trading volume during the breakout rose only slightly and was followed by a period of lower volume. Lower trading volume often accompanies a downtrend, and the price will probably drift lower for an extended period.

## CHART 2-9

Upside Breakout from Downtrend

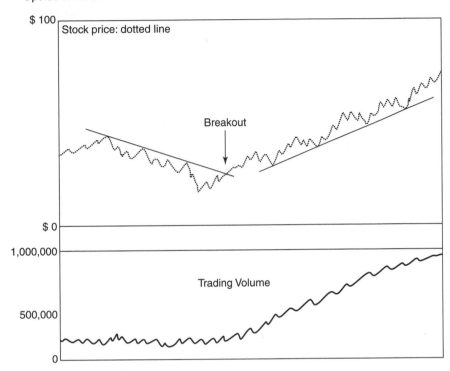

## CHART 2-10

Downside Breakout from Uptrend

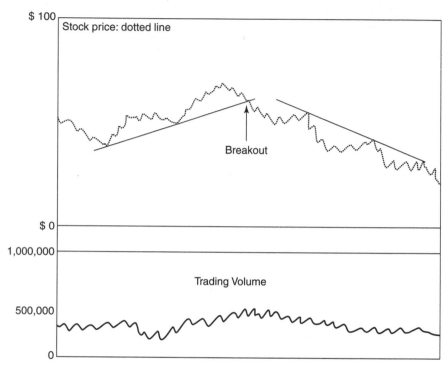

# REVIEW EXERCISE

The last section of this chapter is a review exercise that is comprised
of five charts and related questions. The answer to each question
appears on the page following the chart. After completing this exercise, you will know how well you have learned to analyze the relationships between price patterns, breakouts, and trading volume.

1. Refer to Chart 2-11. This chart shows a stock price breaking out from a trading range to the upside. The breakout is accompanied by a large increase in volume. Is the subsequent price rise likely to develop enough momentum for a significant rise?

**CHART 2-11**

Review Exercise Upside Breakout from Trading Range

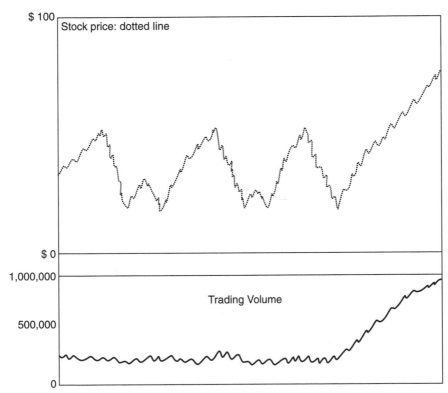

## Answer to Question 1

Yes. The stock price shown in this chart is likely to rise a significant amount because of the large volume increase at the breakout.

2. Refer to Chart 2-12. This chart shows a price breaking out from a symmetrical triangle. Is the price rise likely to be significant?

**CHART 2-12**

Upside Breakout from Symmetrical Triangle

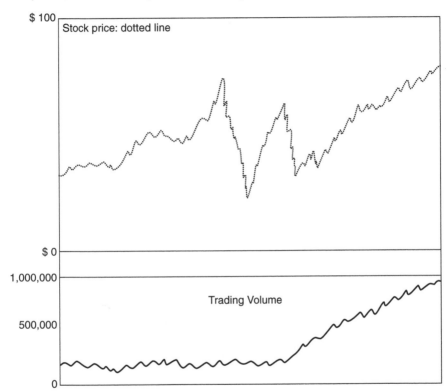

## *Answer to Question 2*

Yes. The price rise is likely to be significant because of the increase in trading volume and because the price has exceeded the highest point in the symmetrical triangle.

3. Refer to Chart 2-13. This chart shows a breakout from a trading range. Is the follow-up action likely to be a large gain in the price?

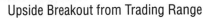

**CHART 2-13**

Upside Breakout from Trading Range

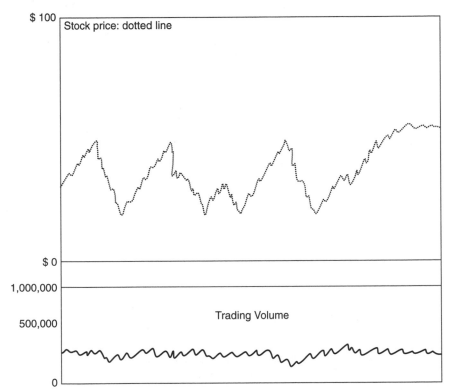

## *Answer to Question 3*

No. The breakout was not accompanied by an increase in trading volume. This shows a lack of conviction on the part of investors at this time. For the stock price to move much higher, some positive new event must occur to arouse enthusiasm in potential buyers.

4. Refer to Chart 2-14. This chart shows a price breakout from a downtrend. Is the uptrend likely to continue a significant distance?

### CHART 2-14

Upside Breakout from Downtrend

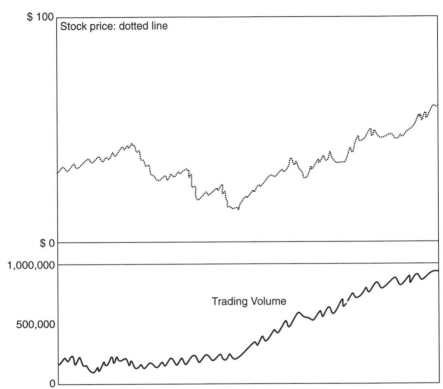

## Answer to Question 4

Yes. The uptrend has good support among investors as indicated by the rise in trading volume. The uptrend will continue unless there is a negative event that makes stock holders eager to sell.

5. Refer to Chart 2-15. In this downside breakout from a symmetrical triangle the trading volume has remained low. Does this imply the decline in price is likely to be small?

CHART 2-15

Downside Breakout from Symmetrical Triangle

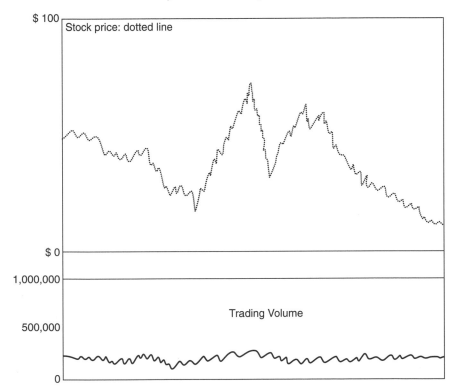

## *Answer to Question 5*

No. The low volume does not imply a small decline in price. The price can continue dropping because of a scarcity of buyers. After a downside breakout from a symmetrical triangle, if the price goes below the lowest point in the triangle, the decline is likely to drift lower for a significant distance.

# 3

# MOVING AVERAGES

## INTRODUCTION

A moving average is shown as a line that smooths out the fluctuations in the stock price. If the stock price is moving up, the moving average line moves up more gradually. If the price is moving down, the average line moves down more gradually. If the stock price is fluctuating up and down, the moving average line moves in a relatively horizontal direction.

There will be periods of time during which the charted price movements of a stock show no discernible pattern. During these time periods you still want to be able to assess the status of a stock. One of the uses of a moving average is to provide the means for making these assessments. By observing the current direction of the moving average line, you can detect whether the stock price is moving up, down, or horizontally.

## CONSTRUCTION OF A MOVING AVERAGE

A moving average is the average of a series of consecutive closing prices. For example, a 10-day moving average is the average of prices from the 10 most recent business days. Tomorrow the oldest price will be dropped from the average and today's price will be added to it. Because the moving average is calculated from past data, it trails the current price. Moving averages are available on stock market and investment Web sites in a wide variety of time periods. Some of the most popular lengths are 5, 10, 20, 50, 100, and 200 days. An investor can select the length of moving average that best suits his or her tempo of trading: short-term, intermediate, or long-term.

## EXPONENTIAL MOVING AVERAGE

There are two types of moving averages. The simple moving average is described above. It gives equal weight to each day's price. The second type is the *exponential moving average* (EMA). It gives extra weight to the more recent days in the sequence, which results in an average that is more up to date than the simple moving average.

## STOCK PRICES AND MOVING AVERAGES

This chapter explains the relationships among stock prices and short and long moving averages. The stock price and moving average illustrations shown in this chapter are similar to some of the thousands of charts that are available on the Internet. The patterns in the eight charts that follow have been idealized to support the instructional purposes of this book. They demonstrate the most significant relationships among stock prices and short- and long-term moving averages. The buy, sell, or hold implications for investors is explained in each case.

### Stock Price Falls Through Moving Average

Refer to Chart 3-1. In this chart, the stock price holds above the moving average for almost a year. When the price falls through the moving average line, this change in the relationship indicates that the price momentum has switched to the downside. An investor

holding this stock who has a profit in it should sell to retain that
capital gain.

## Stock Price Rises above Moving Average

Refer to Chart 3-2. Here the price is fluctuating beneath the moving
average line. When it crosses through the moving average from
below, the change in the relationship indicates that the price
momentum has switched to the upside. In addition, the upward
penetration was accompanied by an increase in trading volume. An
investor contemplating the purchase of this stock can buy it at this
point for the potential capital gain.

## CHART 3-1

Stock Price Falls Through Moving Average

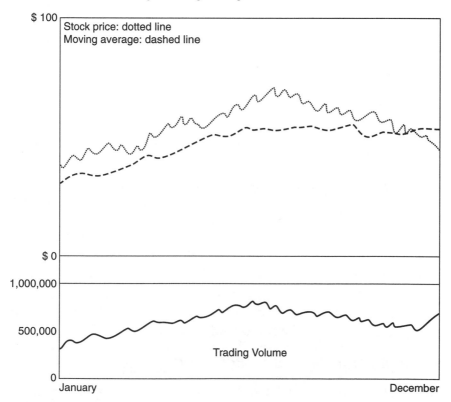

**CHART 3-2**

Stock Price Rises above Moving Average

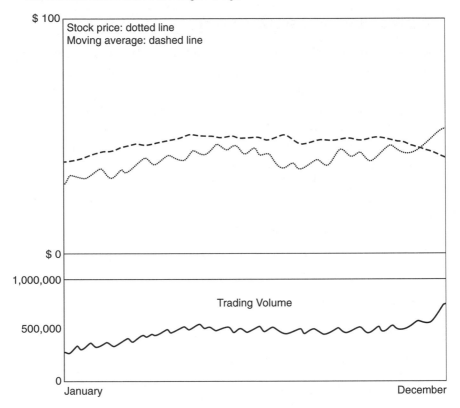

## Moving Average Follows Stock Price Up

Refer to Chart 3-3. In this chart, the moving average line is follow-ing the upward movement in the price. When a moving average follows a sustained price uptrend, this relationship confirms the direction of the price movement. Note also that trading volume has been rising gradually in support of the upward price movement. This chart illustrates a stock that should be bought early in the uptrend and held for the capital gain.

## Moving Average Follows Stock Price Down

Refer to Chart 3-4. Here the moving average line is trailing the price downward. When a moving average follows a price in a sustained

CHART 3-3

Moving Average Follows Stock Price Up

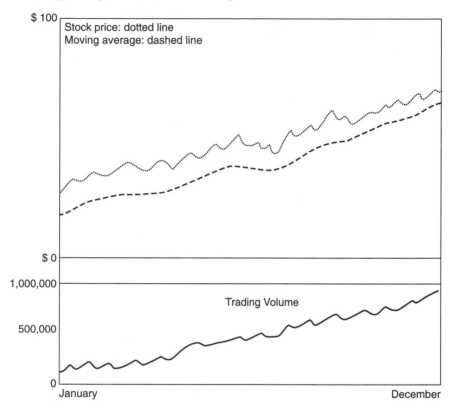

downtrend, this relationship confirms the direction of that price trend. Note that low volume is typical of downtrends. This chart illustrates a stock that should not be bought and, if held, should have been sold as soon as the downtrend was established.

## Short Average Rises above Long Average

Refer to Chart 3-5. This chart shows a change in the relationship between long- and short-term moving average lines. The short-term average was below the long-term average for most of the year. When it crossed above the long-term average at the end of the year, it indicated a positive change in the prospects for the stock. This

**CHART 3-4**

Moving Average Follows Stock Price Down

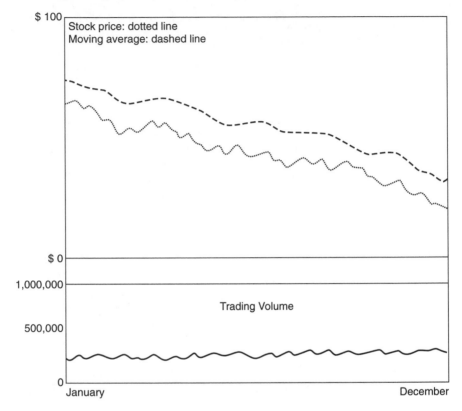

implication applies because the short-term average is reflective of the more recent pricing of the stock. In this case, an investor is alerted to the probability that the stock price may be about to make a move to the upside. The rise in trading volume that coincides with the crossover confirms the change in direction, and an investor can buy for the potential gain.

## *Short Average Falls Through Long Average*

Refer to Chart 3-6. In this chart, the short-term average line tracks the long-term average line and finally crosses down through it. As mentioned with regard to the preceding chart, the short-term aver-

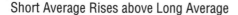

## CHART 3-5

### Short Average Rises above Long Average

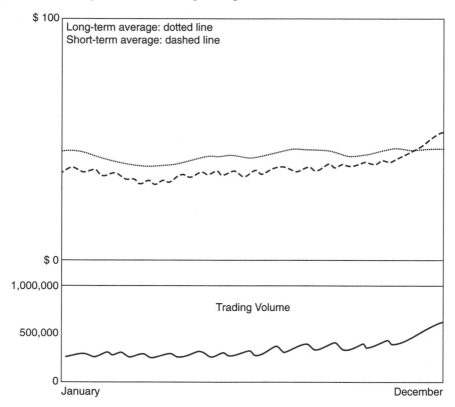

age is more sensitive to changes in the direction of the stock price than the long-term average. In this case, it's likely the stock price will go lower, and if a holder of the stock has a profit, this is the time to take the gain.

### *Stock Price Goes Up Through Short and Long Averages*

Refer to Chart 3-7. This stock price has been below the short- and long-term moving averages. When it moves up through both averages, this surge in the current price is a sign of developing strength and signals there are positive prospects ahead for the stock. Another positive indication is that the trading volume increased

**CHART 3-6**

Short Average Falls Through Long Average

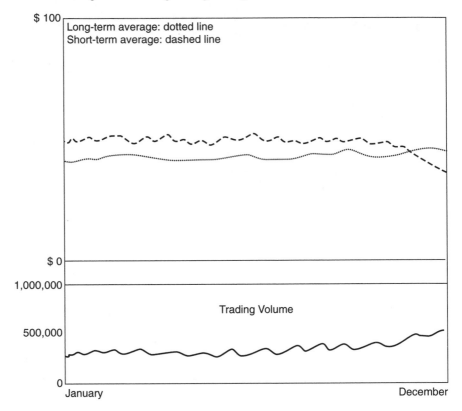

when the stock price broke up through the averages. An investor would be justified in buying this stock for a potential gain.

### Stock Price Goes Down Through Short And Long Averages

Refer to Chart 3-8. This is the opposite of the preceding chart and has negative implication because current pricing is more relevant than previous prices. Here the stock price goes down through both the short- and long-term moving averages. This double penetration signals a potentially significant decline in the stock price. An investor who has a profit in this stock should sell to preserve his or her gain.

## C H A R T 3-7

### Stock Price Goes Up Through Short and Long Averages

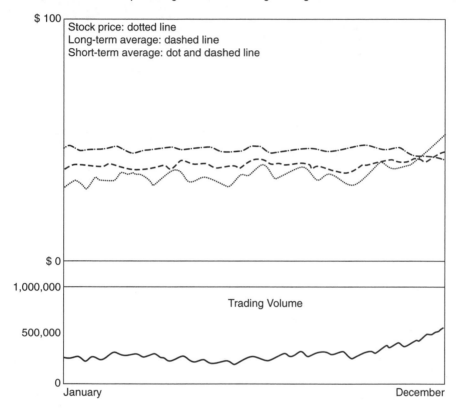

## CHART 3-8

### Stock Price Goes Down Through Short And Long Averages

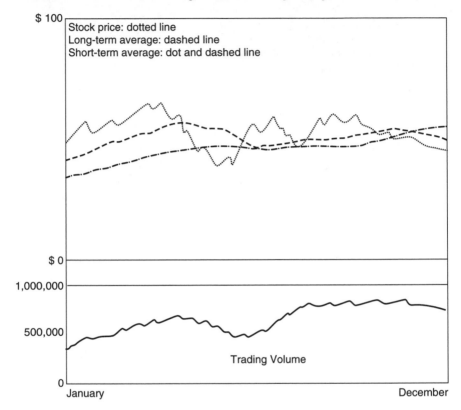

Stock price: dotted line
Long-term average: dashed line
Short-term average: dot and dashed line

Trading Volume

## REVIEW EXERCISE

This review exercise presents three questions to help you check your knowledge of the relationships between stock prices and a moving average of any length.

1. Refer to Chart 3-9. The moving average has been trailing the stock price upward. Does this relationship confirm the uptrend in the stock price?

**C H A R T   3-9**

Question 1

## Answer to Question 1

Yes. A moving average that follows a stock price upward is confirming the trend and indicates the stock can be held for a potential gain.

2. Refer to Chart 3-10. Here the stock price has dropped through the moving average. Is this change in the relationship a matter of concern to an investor?

## CHART 3-10

Question 2

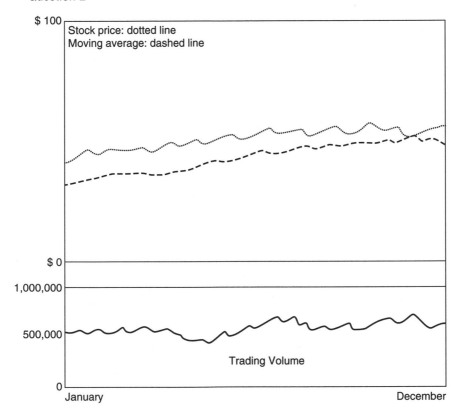

## Answer to Question 2

Yes. When the stock price goes below the moving average it indicates a change in the stock price momentum to the downside. An investor holding this stock can take this event as a sell signal even though the volume of trading has not increased.

3. Refer to Chart 3-11. This stock price has been below the moving average for most of the year. At the end of the year, it goes up through the average on an increase in volume. Can an investor take this event as a buy signal?

**CHART 3-11**

Question 3

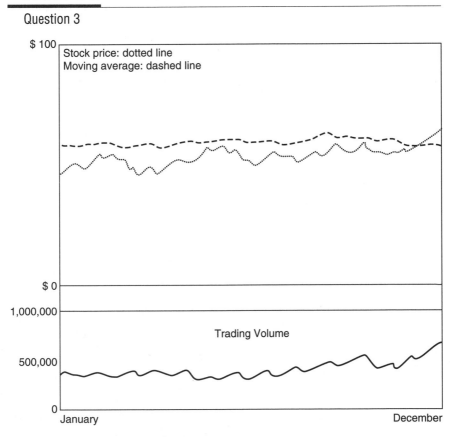

## Answer to Question 3

Yes. This is a buy signal and an investor can buy for a potential capital gain.

# 4

# PORTFOLIO MANAGEMENT

## INTRODUCTION

You are now familiar with the basic concepts of technical analysis. The next objective is to help you learn how to use these concepts to manage your portfolio. Table 4-1 provides a framework for understanding the principles of portfolio management. Later in this chapter you will learn how technical analysis can assist you in selecting stocks and funds to construct a suitable portfolio and manage it through changing market conditions.

## DEALING WITH MARKET PHASES

In order to manage a portfolio effectively, it's important to be aware of each market phase. In the *bull market* phase, stock prices follow a long-term trend upward with only short-term moves downward. In a *bear market*, stock prices follow a long-term trend downward with only short-term moves upward. In a *range-bound market*, stock prices move up and down within a limited vertical range and there is no clear direction to the market as a whole.

The bull market phase is the appropriate time for the aggressive approach of buying growth stocks and funds for large capital gains. In a range-bound market, investors should buy growth stocks and income funds for a balance between capital gains and

**TABLE 4-1**

A Framework and Rationale for Portfolio Management

| Market Phase | Bull Market | Range-Bound Market | Bear Market |
|---|---|---|---|
| Management Style | Aggressive | Balanced | Conservative |
| Portfolio Content | Growth Stocks and Funds | Growth Stocks and Income Funds | Bonds and Preferred Stocks |
| Objectives | Large Capital Gains | Capital Gains and High Income | Preserve Capital |

income flow. The reason to take this balanced approach in a range-bound market is that growth stocks grow more slowly during that phase and the extra income from the funds compensates for the slower growth. In a bear market, when stock prices are declining, a conservative style of investing is appropriate. Conservative investing requires buying investments that preserve capital (for example, preferred stocks and bonds, which respectively pay dividends and interest and return the invested capital at the call or maturity dates).

Some investors are inclined to stay with one of the three management styles through bull, bear, and range-bound markets. This strategy works well less than half the time. Aggressive investors who own growth stocks see capital losses in bear markets because most growth stocks fall along with the market averages. Conservative investors who rely mostly on preferred stocks and bonds miss out on capital gains, which are plentiful in a bull market. And the balanced style investor gets only minimum gains in a bull market and may lose most of those gains in a bear market. In view of these harsh market realities, it is evident that style flexibility is the key ingredient for getting better than average results in the stock market.

Another requirement for getting improved results is the ability to recognize bull or bear markets in their early stages. To detect the start of a bull market, look for bottoming patterns and starting uptrends. When you see these, it's time to switch to a more aggressive style. To spot a bear market coming, look for topping out patterns and starting downtrends. When you see these, it's time to switch to a more conservative style. And when the market averages have been trendless for several months, it's time to switch to a more balanced style if you have been aggressive in the preceding period.

## SELECTING STOCKS AND FUNDS FOR AN AGGRESSIVE PORTFOLIO

Now let's consider how to use the concepts of technical analysis to find stocks and funds suitable for an aggressive portfolio. First, let's review how you would find investments to produce large capital gains. To do this, look for the three types of price patterns predictive of major price movements to the upside. These are the inverted head and shoulders, the double bottom, and the rounding bottom. Let's start with one of the most significant bottoming patterns.

### Inverted Head and Shoulders

Refer to Chart 4-1 and review the inverted head and shoulders pattern. This pattern is predictive of a large capital gain. It develops at bottoms in a three-phase process. Phase one is the round bottom of the first shoulder. At this point, the price has fallen a long distance and some of the stockholders sell out because they are unnerved by the decline. Phase two is the head. While the head is forming, many stockholders sell in panic as they watch prices sink to the lowest level seen in a long time. Phase three is the second shoulder. As the price starts to drop again, the last few holdouts give up and sell their shares to knowledgeable new buyers who have reason to believe the company will soon be on the road to recovery. Now the stage is set for a major move upward and the breakout on increased volume gives the buy signal.

**CHART 4-1**

Inverted Head and Shoulders

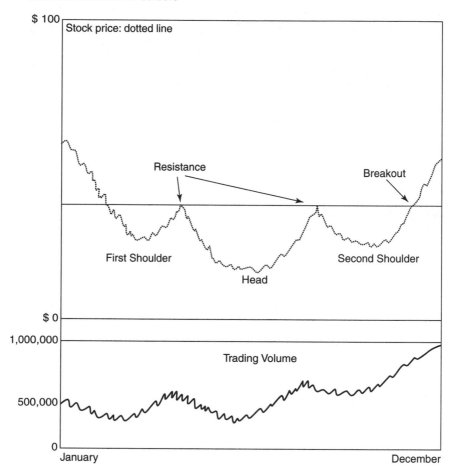

## Double Bottom

Refer to Chart 4-2. A double bottom is another price pattern that may develop after a long decline in the price of a stock. As the first bottom forms, many stockholders are frightened by the lowest prices seen in a long time, and some of them sell out. The rise from the first bottom meets resistance because there is still a lot of bad publicity about the company, and potential buyers believe the

## CHART 4-2

Double Bottom

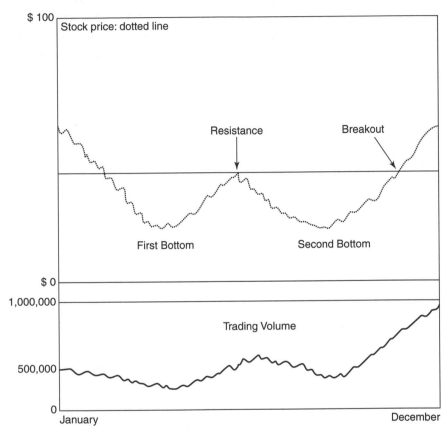

quick price rise is not justified. As the price goes back down to the previous low, more stockholders panic and sell their shares.

Meanwhile, some well-informed investors are hearing that the company is entering a recovery phase and they are becoming convinced they are getting a bargain at this low level. With the selling exhausted, the stock is ready for a strong rally, and the price breaks out above the resistance level on increased volume, which provides a buy signal for additional investors who believe this is the beginning of a long-term uptrend.

## *Rounding Bottom*

Refer to Chart 4-3. This pattern is the rounding bottom. The first part of this pattern is a slow, drifting downtrend. During this downtrend the patience of many stockholders is exhausted, and more and more of them succumb to the fear that the company cannot deal with its financial problems. There is no good news about the company, but as the price reaches bargain levels some knowl-

**CHART 4-3**

Rounding Bottom

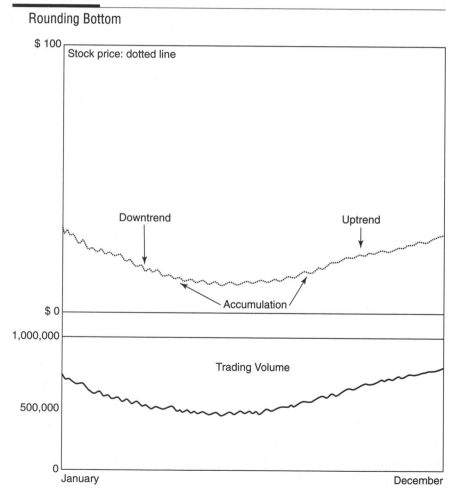

edgeable investors and others attracted by the low price decide to take advantage of the situation. They accumulate all the shares offered by the discouraged stockholders.

The length of the accumulation period is dependent on the number of shares outstanding. The more shares that are available for sale, the longer the time that will be required to accumulate them. As this process continues, the demand from new buyers gradually overcomes the supply and an uptrend begins. There is no breakout point in this pattern. The increasing volume and the establishment of an uptrend provide the signs that the price of the stock is headed toward higher levels over the long term.

## CHART 4-4

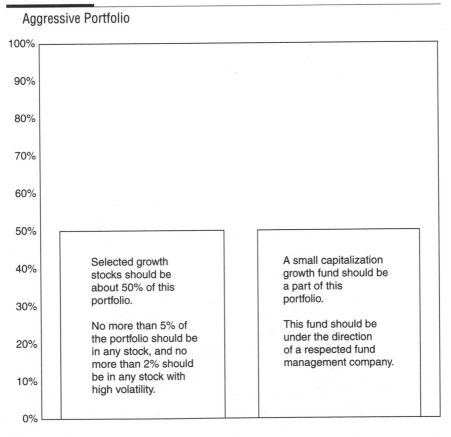

Aggressive Portfolio

Selected growth stocks should be about 50% of this portfolio.

No more than 5% of the portfolio should be in any stock, and no more than 2% should be in any stock with high volatility.

A small capitalization growth fund should be a part of this portfolio.

This fund should be under the direction of a respected fund management company.

Selecting stocks based on any of these three bottoming patterns provides an excellent opportunity to make large price gains under favorable market conditions.

In addition to individual stocks, a small capitalization growth fund is an appropriate investment to have in an aggressive portfolio. Ask your broker to give you the names and symbols of several of these funds. You can then look them up on www.finance.yahoo.com to see which ones have any of the bottoming patterns described above.

### An Aggressive Portfolio

Refer to Chart 4-4 for a sample of a mixture of investments that is appropriate for an aggressive portfolio. This mix would be most suitable during a bull stock market, when large capital gains are common for growth stocks.

## A BALANCED PORTFOLIO

Refer to Chart 4-5. The portfolio style that has a balance between the objectives of capital gains and income flow is the next one to consider. The amount of assets to devote to each of these objectives does not have to be equal. You should decide if you want to place more emphasis on capital gains or on income flow.

The first step in developing this type of portfolio is to select growth stocks for large capital gains. This can be done by identifying bottoming patterns as was done for the aggressive portfolio. In addition to those three patterns, others that can produce gains are the ascending and symmetrical triangles. These price patterns and formations present opportunities for making capital gains in a balanced portfolio while the market averages are range bound.

The next step is to chose some investments that can deliver high income flow. Here are samples of these types of investments, which are known as closed-end funds.

### World Income Funds

These are mutual funds that make investments anywhere in the world. These funds are managed by investment banks and have the

## CHART 4-5

Balanced Portfolio

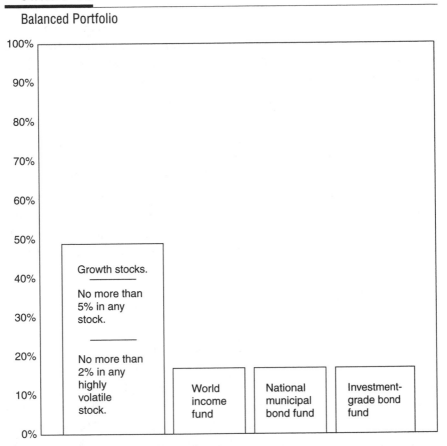

stated objective of delivering a high and reliable income flow. A list of these funds can be found in *Barron's* weekly magazine in the section titled, "Closed End Funds." Details on the composition of each fund can be found at www.cefa.com.

When you have some time to do research, go to that address. (Enter a fund symbol, click on the triangle icon, review the performance data screen, and, for more detailed information on the content of the fund, click on "Click here for more information on this fund."

These closed-end funds trade like stocks. Daily charts on these funds are published on www.finance.yahoo.com and they can be analyzed in the same manner as individual stocks.

### National Municipal Bond Funds

Another type of high-income investment is the municipal bond fund. These are listed in Barron's closed-end fund section under the heading of "National Muni Bond Funds." Each of these funds contains municipal bonds from 40 or more different states. This broad representation makes these funds safer than funds containing bonds issued from just one state. These funds are managed by investment banks that specialize in bonds.

By researching the information at www.cefa.com you can learn which states' bonds are contained in any of these funds. The yields for all these funds are listed in *Barron's* weekly magazine along with the premium over, or discount from, the current price. In selecting a fund from this list, choosing a high-yielding fund selling at a discount is more likely to be a better investment than choosing a fund that yields less and sells at a premium. The best time to buy these funds is when interest rates are high.

### Investment-Grade Bond Funds

A third type of closed-end fund that can produce a high income flow is listed in Barron's closed-end funds section under the title "Investment Grade Bond Funds." These funds contain high-grade bonds as ranked by Standard & Poor's, Moody's, and Fitch bond-rating services. The higher-yielding funds selling at a discount, if bought when interest rates are high, are a suitable addition to a balanced portfolio.

Refer to Chart 4-5 for the types of stocks and funds that could be included in this style of portfolio. Which specific stocks and funds you choose should be based on your research and investment objectives.

Since a balanced portfolio is subject to decline in value during a bear market, when you see the stock market averages starting into a downtrend, it's time to switch to a conservative portfolio.

## A CONSERVATIVE PORTFOLIO

The objectives of a conservative portfolio are to preserve capital and receive income with a minimum level of risk. Consequently, the investments in this type of portfolio should be among those that are the safest available.

## Zero Coupon Bonds

Zero coupon bonds are one of the safest investments because they are backed by the full faith and credit of the United States government. Zero coupon bonds are bought at a discount, and, when mature, pay the investor full face value, thus providing a capital gain. The amount of gain depends on the size of the discount from face value. If you think you might need to sell some of the bonds before they mature, buy short-term bonds to minimize price fluctuations while you are holding them. These bonds can be bought

**CHART 4-6**

Conservative Portfolio

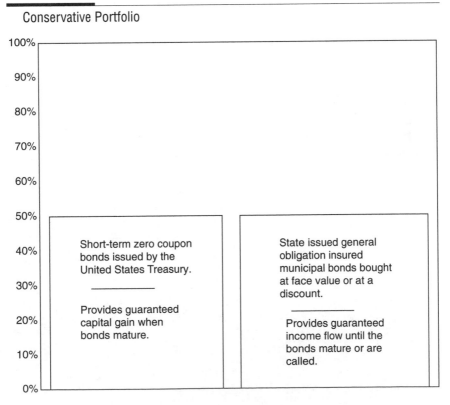

| | |
|---|---|
| Short-term zero coupon bonds issued by the United States Treasury. | State issued general obligation insured municipal bonds bought at face value or at a discount. |
| Provides guaranteed capital gain when bonds mature. | Provides guaranteed income flow until the bonds mature or are called. |

through your broker or directly from the United States Treasury Web site whose address is www.treasurydirect.gov.

## General Obligation Municipal Bonds

Another type of investment with a high degree of safety is the general obligation municipal bond issued by state governments. The term *general obligation* refers to a bond that is backed by the financial resources of the state that issues it. In addition, these bonds can be insured by one of the bond insurers (Ambac Financial Group, MBIA Insurance Group, or Financial Guaranty Insurance Company). A major benefit of municipal bonds is that there is little or no tax on the interest payments, depending on which state you live in. Your broker can give you the details and help you find the safest bonds. When interest rates are high, you may be able to buy these bonds at a discount. Don't pay a premium over the par value because you would have a capital loss when the bond matures.

Now look at Chart 4-6 to see the types of investments appropriate for a conservative portfolio.

## REVIEW EXERCISE

Here is a review exercise that is comprised of six questions and associated charts.

1. Refer to Chart 4-7. True or false? This type of inverted head and shoulders pattern occurs at the end of an extended drop in price and provides an opportunity for a large capital gain.

## CHART 4-7

Inverted Head and Shoulders

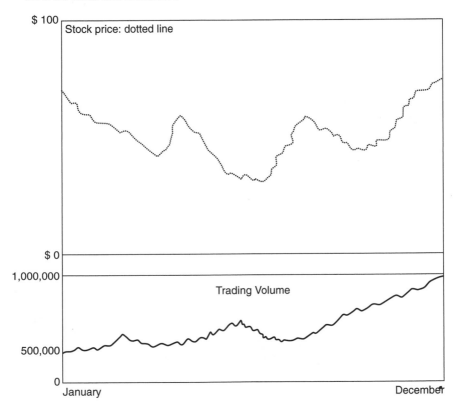

## *Answer to Question 1*

True. An inverted head and shoulders pattern may occur after a long decline in price and signals that a reversal has occurred leading to the opportunity for a major capital gain after a breakout on increased volume.

2. Refer to Chart 4-8. True or false? Since there are only two phases in this double bottom pattern, it is likely to result in a smaller capital gain than the inverted head and shoulders pattern.

## CHART 4-8

### Double Bottom

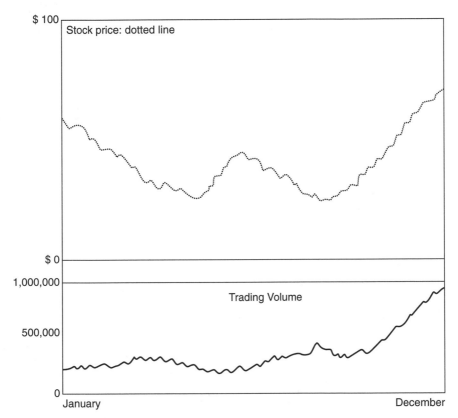

## Answer to Question 2

False. A double bottom is one of three bottoming patterns of equal potential to produce major capital gains. If there were a difference in the amount of gain to be expected, it would depend on the size of the patterns and time consumed in creating them rather than the shape.

3. Refer to Chart 4-9. True or false? An accumulation pattern is usually a smoothly rounding formation because the financial condition of the company is changing gradually from very bad to a recovery situation. Well-informed investors become aware of this transformation and this motivates them to accumulate all of the shares offered for sale.

## CHART 4-9

Rounding Bottom

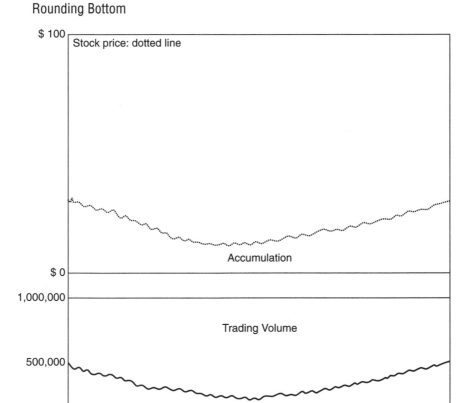

## *Answer to Question 3*

True. Well-informed investors know when a company's prospects are improving gradually and are willing to accumulate all the shares offered at bargain prices.

4. Refer to Chart 4-10. Is this the type of portfolio suitable for young investors while the stock market is in a bullish phase?

### CHART 4-10

Conservative Portfolio

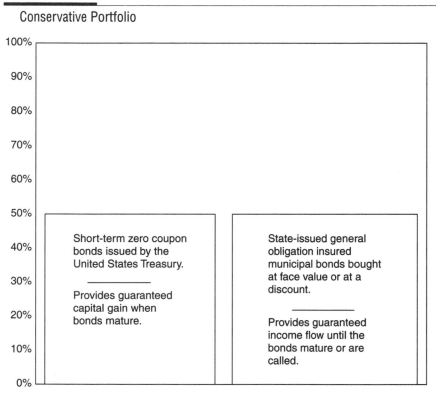

## Answer to Question 4

No. A portfolio consisting of bonds is not suitable for young investors while the market is in a bullish phase or in a market going sideways. To build their wealth, young investors should have growth stocks and growth funds for the capital gains they can produce.

5. Refer to Chart 4-11. Is this the type of portfolio suitable for retirees during a bear market?

**CHART 4-11**

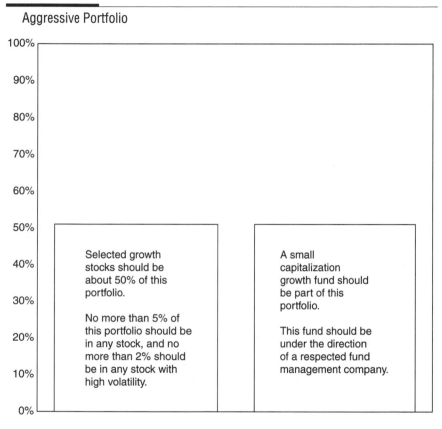

Aggressive Portfolio

Selected growth stocks should be about 50% of this portfolio.

No more than 5% of this portfolio should be in any stock, and no more than 2% should be in any stock with high volatility.

A small capitalization growth fund should be part of this portfolio.

This fund should be under the direction of a respected fund management company.

## Answer to Question 5

No, retirees should be holding assets that produce guaranteed capital gains and income, such as government bonds and other low-risk investments.

6. Refer to Chart 4-12. Is this the type of portfolio for investors seeking a balanced combination of growth of capital and high income flow?

## CHART 4-12

### Balanced Portfolio

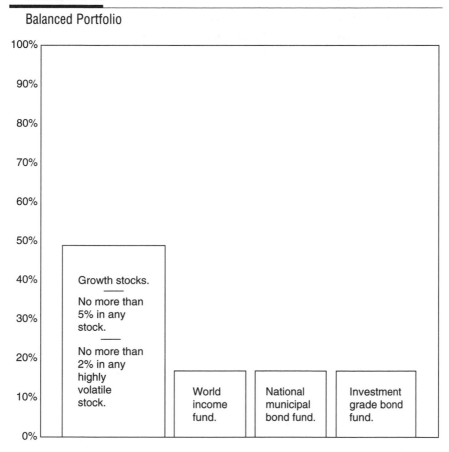

## Answer to Question 6

Yes. This type of portfolio has two complementary objectives. Growth stocks provide the potential for large capital gains over the long run. These investments are suitable for investors willing to accept a reasonable level of risk to achieve those rewards. And diversified funds that produce a steady flow of income provide a new source of investment capital as the income accumulates.

# 5

# TECHNICAL ANALYSIS
# AND THE STOCK MARKET

## INTRODUCTION

Each investor should deal with the market in a way that fits with his or her personal inclinations. If you prefer fast-paced action and are willing and able to devote a lot of time to the stock market, trading actively may be appropriate for you. If you are patient and content with a leisurely pace in life, the buy and hold strategy may work for you. Or perhaps your lifestyle is somewhere in between—wanting immediate gratification and waiting patiently for your satisfactions. If so, it may suit you well to buy and sell in the intermediate time periods. This chapter describes how technical analysis can be helpful in each of these three time frames.

## ACTIVE TRADING

Trading stocks actively can be exciting, intriguing, and rewarding. Or it can be stressful, emotionally overwhelming, and produce heavy losses. The investors most likely to succeed at this endeavor are those who have learned to conquer fear and greed and developed the temperament to survive in all market phases. A reliable alternate income will help the active trader keep the stress level within manageable limits. The investors most likely to fail are those who want to use the market as a gambling casino to get rich quickly.

If you want to be an active trader, here are some suggestions to help you get started.

1.  Conduct a dry run for a month, making 30 to 40 imaginary purchases and sales.

2.  Keep a record of your reason for making each purchase and sale and the amounts of your profits and losses.

3.  At the end of the month, tally the results. If you show a loss, analyze your reasoning and work to improve your evaluation process. Do this for several months until your profits exceed your loses by a significant amount.

4.  Before you start actual trading, open a cash account with a broker who charges very small commissions. This will keep those costs to a minimum and the monthly statements will allow you to stay abreast of your progress. Put only that amount of cash into this account so that even if lost, it will not force you to reduce your lifestyle.

## HOW TECHNICAL ANALYSIS CAN HELP

The following suggestions will help you to start trading. Watch some financial shows on television in which stock quotes are shown live at the bottom of the screen. Look for stock symbols that trade frequently. Make a list of 10 or more symbols in the price range of interest to you. Then go to www.finance.yahoo.com and check the price patterns on those stocks. Look for an uptrend that is just starting, with two or three ascending bottoms. Use a ruler to see if bottoms can be aligned to identify an uptrend. If so, make a note of that symbol. Then find some more ascending stock price bottoms that pass the ruler test. After you find several stocks that are in uptrends, you can then monitor the stock price quote tape on a financial television show or on a computer to decide which ones have the price actions that look most promising. After you make those selections, you will be ready to take on the challenges of trading actively.

Knowing how to trade an uptrend is an important aspect of trading. The best time to buy is after the stock price has risen a little way from the trendline. When to sell is a matter of judgment because there is no reliable way to predict where the short-term rises will end.

Refer to Chart 5-1 for an illustration of the buy and sell areas in a typical uptrend.

An alternate method is to go back to www.Finance.Yahoo.com, pull up the same price charts, and add in a medium length moving average. For each stock, observe how the price relates to the moving average. Try to find several stocks whose prices have bounced up from their average two or more times. (Some stock prices bounce up

## CHART 5-1

Trading an Uptrend

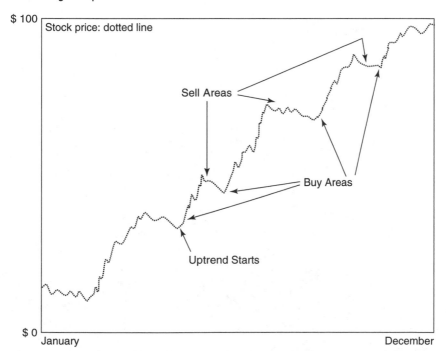

from their moving averages and there is no straight trendline to use as a reference.) Refer to Chart 5-2 to see how to use a moving average as a reference guideline for making trades.

Another approach is to look for trading range patterns. By identifying the support level, you have the potential purchase areas; and by identifying the resistance level, you have the potential selling areas to complete the transactions. Again, it's a practical trading tactic to wait for a small bounce up from a support level before buying. Also, wait for a small decline from a resistance level before making your sale to reduce the chance of selling a stock just before it makes an upside breakout. Refer to Chart 5-3 to see a representation of how this can be done in the most effective manner.

Wide trading ranges present the opportunity to make large profits on each buy and sell transaction. Narrow trading ranges

## CHART 5-2

### Trading a Moving Average

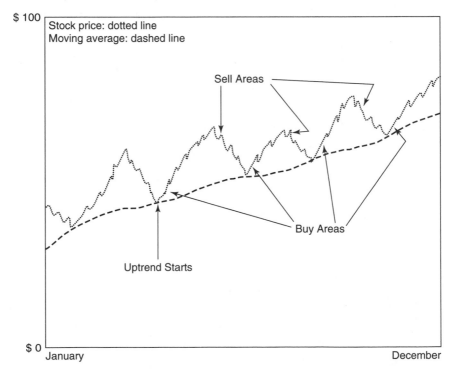

## CHART 5-3

Trading a Trading Range

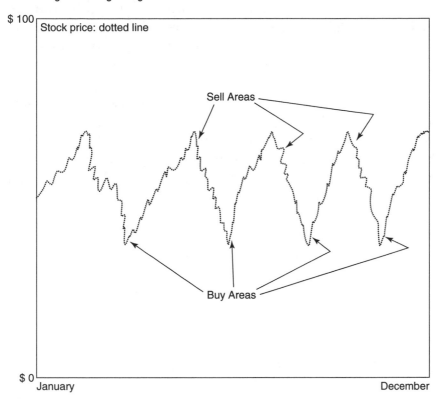

also provide good opportunities for profits if they last a long time because they allow a large number of transactions. Given a choice, it's preferable to trade the wider range because there is no reliable way to predict how long a trading range will last.

Trading ranges are most likely to develop when the stock market is facing a mix of positive and negative factors in the economy and it cannot develop momentum to move up or down for an extended period of time. This is known as a *range-bound market*, as distinct from bull and bear markets. It's therefore a good idea to learn how to trade within wide, medium, and narrow trading ranges because there will be extended periods of time when the stock market will be range bound.

Another productive activity is to look for ascending and symmetrical triangles. The breakout from an ascending triangle will be to the upside most of the time, so identifying this type of triangle can be worthwhile. Once a breakout to the upside on increased volume has occurred, the extent of the rise will usually be at least equal to the height of the triangle. Refer to Chart 5-4 to see an example of this relationship.

Breakouts from symmetrical triangles can occur to the upside or the downside. The main clue to which direction the price will go after a breakout is the direction from which the price approaches the triangle. If the price rose up into the triangle, the breakout will usually be to the upside. In this case, the triangle has served as a continuation formation.

## CHART 5-4

Trading an Ascending Triangle

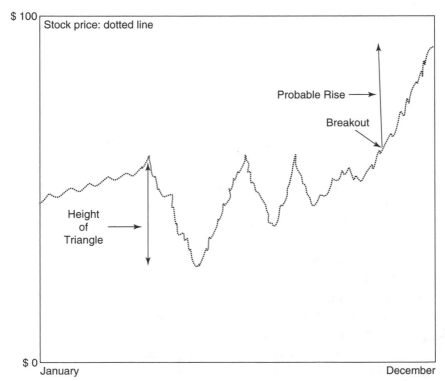

## CHART 5-5

### Trading Symmetrical Triangles

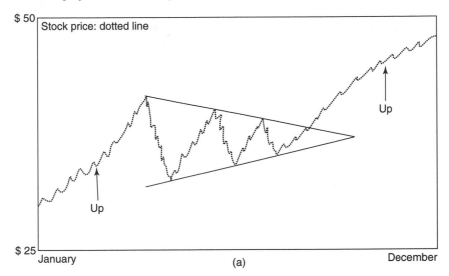

(a)

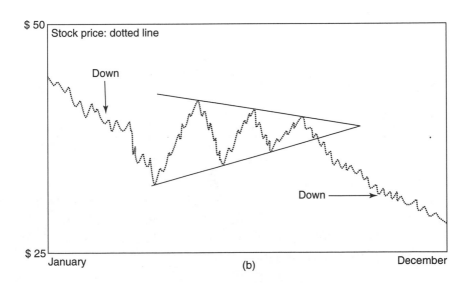

(b)

**CHART 5-6**

Uptrend and Topping Out Pattern

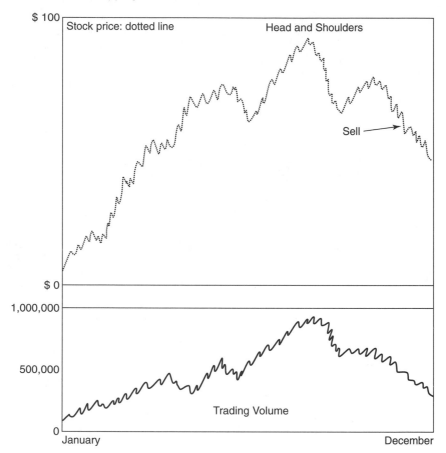

Similarly, if the price comes down into a triangle, the breakout will probably be to the downside, in which case the triangle has again been a continuation formation. In both cases, you should wait for the breakout before making any decision. Refer to Chart 5-5 (a) and (b) to see these two situations.

## BUY AND HOLD INVESTING

Now let's consider the approach that requires patience: buying and holding for the long term. This strategy works well in a strong bull market, but can produce extensive paper loses in a bear market. So the actual holding period has to be subject to market conditions and to the changing fortunes of the company, as reflected in the price of the stock. These changing conditions can be detected through technical analysis. If you are holding a stock in a long-term uptrend, it's prudent to be on the watch for a topping out pattern. Continuous alertness is necessary because the danger in the buy and hold strategy is that, after a long and rewarding rise in price, you may become emotionally attached to a stock and convinced it can only go up. The old adage, "What goes up, must come down" applies to the market. Enjoy the ride, but be ready to sell when a topping out pattern or a breakout to the downside tells you the ride is over. Refer to Chart 5-6 for an illustration of a long uptrend ending in a topping out pattern.

Investors using the buy and hold approach should be ready to make changes in their portfolios to deal with a bear market. The start of a bear market can be detected by watching the market averages. When it appears that the averages have established downtrends, a switch from an aggressive or balanced portfolio to a conservative one is an effective tactic for preserving capital. Charts of the market averages are shown daily on financial television stations and in many newspapers.

## INTERMEDIATE-TERM TRADING

Technical analysis can be very helpful to the intermediate-term trader. Very few stocks follow an uninterrupted uptrend from a bottoming pattern to a topping pattern. There are often some variations and intervening patterns along the way. For example, a price in an uptrend may move into a trading range. Ranges with a large distance between the bottom and the top present opportunities for an investor trading in the intermediate term to make gains.

First, the investor can buy near the support level and sell near the resistance level a few times. Next, if the price breaks out to the upside on increased volume, the trader can buy back in during the breakout and hold on for a price rise that will probably be at least as large as the distance between the top and bottom of the range. Finally, after the upward price move runs its course, the trader should wait to see if an ascending or symmetrical triangle forms. If so, the trader can continue holding in anticipation of a breakout to the upside because many triangles are continuation formations.

Refer to the triangle price pattern in Chart 5-5 (a). An alert investor can find sequences like this once or twice a year, which can add up to a sizeable capital gain. Another tactic is to buy a stock in the early stage of an uptrend and hold on until it ends. In the course of a year, there are usually several stocks in intermediate-length uptrends that provide opportunities for significant profits.

## REVIEW EXERCISE

1. Refer to Charts 5-7 (a) and (b). Two trading ranges of different widths are shown in these charts. Chart 5-7 (a) is narrow and Chart 5-7 (b) is about twice as wide. To make the greater amount of profit, which of these two stocks would an experienced trader choose to trade?

## CHART 5-7

### Question 1

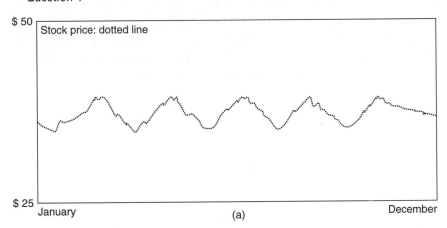

$ 50

Stock price: dotted line

$ 25

January                                    (a)                        December

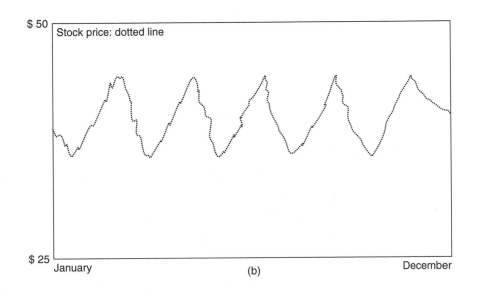

$ 50

Stock price: dotted line

$ 25

January                                    (b)                        December

## Answer to Question 1

An experienced trader should be able to make approximately twice as much profit by trading the stock depicted in Chart 5-7 (b). Both stocks provide five opportunities to buy and sell for a profit, but the profit for each transaction would be about twice as large for the stock in Chart 5-7 (b) as for the one in Chart 5-7 (a).

2. Refer to Charts 5-8 (a) and (b). Investors A and B each have been holding their stock for a year. They bought at $20 a share and they each have a profit of $15 per share. They are both planning to keep holding because they have done so well. Which investor is likely to have more profit at the end of the next quarter?

## CHART 5-8

Question 2

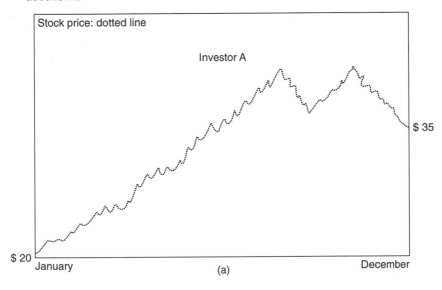

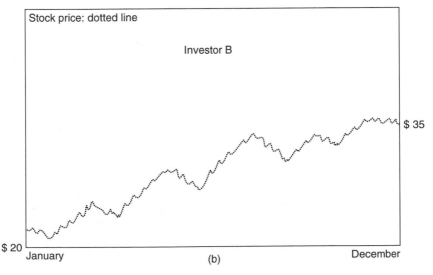

## Answer to Question 2

Investor B is likely to have more profit at the end of the next quarter because the stock in Chart 5-8(b) is in a continuing uptrend. Investor A is likely to have less profit because the stock in Chart 5-8 (a) has made a double top and is likely to decline in the coming months.

3. Refer to Charts 5-9 (a) and (b). Investors A and B each have a stock that has formed an ascending triangle. Each stock price has broken out to the upside. Which investor is likely to get the larger profit from the upward price moves that follow the breakouts?

## CHART 5-9

### Question 3

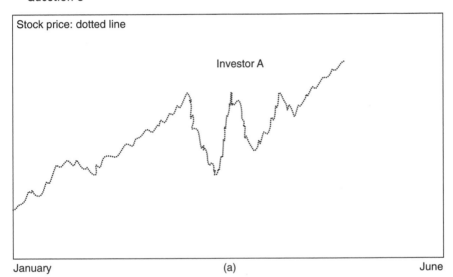

Stock price: dotted line

Investor A

January                          (a)                          June

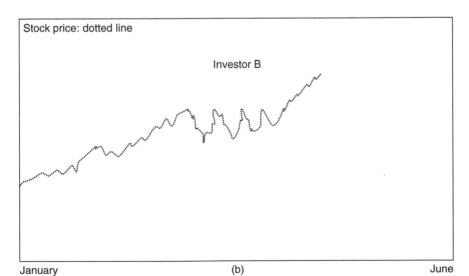

Stock price: dotted line

Investor B

January                          (b)                          June

## *Answer to Question 3*

Investor A is likely to get the larger price gain. The triangle formed by Investor A's stock price is about twice as large as the one formed by Investor B's stock price. A price move following a breakout from an ascending triangle is usually equal to or greater than the height of the triangle. The price move from the triangle in Chart 5-9 (a) should be at least twice as large as that of the price move from the the triangle in Chart 5-9 (b).

4. Refer to Chart 5-10. In this chart the price of the stock is trending upward in a series of up and down short-term price moves. A trader can try to buy at the bottom point of each small price move or he or she can wait until the price has started moving up from the trendline. True or false? It's safer to wait for the bounce up from the trendline than to try to buy at the lowest point.

## CHART 5-10

### Question 4

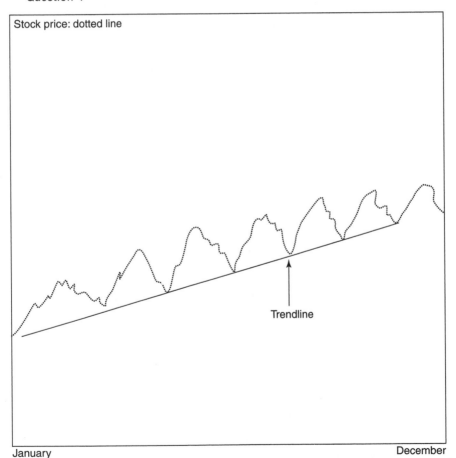

Stock price: dotted line

Trendline

January                                                                December

## *Answer to Question 4*

True. It's safer to wait for the bounce up from the trendline because a downside breakout from a trendline can occur without warning.

CHAPTER

# 6

# TECHNICAL ANALYSIS
# AND THE INTERNET

## INTRODUCTION

This chapter takes you on a guided tour of some of the Web sites containing information that is helpful in performing a technical analysis. The sites to be reviewed were selected because they display comprehensive information, they're easy to use, and much of what they provide is free. And these sites can quote stock prices at any time.

## YAHOO! FINANCE WEB SITE

This is one of the best sites because it provides a great amount of free, helpful information. It contains charts on thousands of stocks and funds, showing historical prices for 5 days, 3 months, 6 months, 1 year, 2 years, and 5 years. The charts also show daily trading volumes and the average trading volume over the preceding 3 months. The price performance of several stocks can be shown and compared over a variety of time periods.

When you have access to a computer and some free time, you can take the following educational tour of the Yahoo! Finance Web site. Start by entering the Web address www.finance.yahoo.com into the search slot of your service provider or your home page.

After arriving at the first screen, enter a stock symbol in the search slot. For example, enter the symbol of General Electric company. What you would see after you enter "GE" and click the "Go" button is a summary chart that includes the following items:

- The price of the latest trade in GE
- The price range during the day
- The range of prices during the last year
- The trading volume for the day
- The average daily trading volume for the last 3 months (this average trading volume is important because it is a benchmark against which daily volumes can be compared)

Also shown at the bottom of the left-hand column in this display chart is the estimated price target for GE in the coming 12 months. There are other items in this display, but for our purposes, the main value of this site is found by clicking on the phrase "Technical Analysis" on the left side of the screen.

The chart that appears on the screen shows 1 year of price and trading volume fluctuations. Additional choices are available, such as the following options:

- A longer or shorter time period
- Moving averages: short, medium length, long, simple, and exponential
- Other indicators and overlays of interest to technical analysts

Another search slot above the chart lets you compare the price performance of General Electric against several other stocks or indexes.

Here are some activities you may find of interest. Pull up the technical analysis chart for General Electric or a stock of your choosing and scan it to see if there are any price patterns you are familiar with. Then select both a short and long exponential moving average (EMA) and look for relationships between them and the stock price. After you have reviewed these items, you may want to explore some of the other options offered by the Web site.

## CLEAR STATION WEB SITE

This is another excellent site for technical information. To get there, enter the following address in the search slot of your service provider or your home page, www.clearstation.com.

In the Clear Station home page search slot, enter the symbol of a stock of interest to you. Then click "Go." Here's an explanation of the display and a preview of the information that will be available on the stock you enter.

The title of the display is "3 Point View." This title refers to the content of the column on the left side of the screen. Scroll down and you'll see three headings: "Technicals," "Fundamentals," and "Community." We will review the technical segment.

Under this heading, the first item is an arrow pointing up or down to indicate whether the stock price is above or below the 50-day exponential moving average. An arrow pointing up means the prospects for the stock are positive for the intermediate future. An arrow pointing down means the prospects are negative.

In the chart to the right there is a pink line representing a 50-day exponential moving average and a green line representing a 13-day exponential moving average. The relationship of each of these averages to the stock price is indicated under the phrase, "Last Price Quote is."

The percentage figures given indicate how far the latest price is above or below each of the averages. If the price is above both averages, it has positive implications. If it is below both averages, it is a negative sign. If the price is above one and below the other, the implication is indefinite. At some point, the price will move above or below both averages and the situation will be clarified.

The next item is titled, "RS Rating." RS stands for relative strength. The number shown indicates the level of strength relative to other stocks. For example, the number 75 indicates a relative strength higher than 75 percent of other stocks. Any number below 50 indicates weakness relative to other stocks. The chart shown is known as a bar chart because vertical bars are used to represent the price range during the day or other time period. The volume of trading is shown in a separate section at the bottom of the chart.

In the chart the letter "E" is shown within a red triangle that points up or down. The E stands for earnings and the triangle points up if the earnings were higher than reported previously, or down if the earnings were lower. If the company is paying a dividend, a "D" is shown inside a blue box. The amount of dividend paid is indicated below the box.

If the stock market is open, you can get an updated chart and all related data by clicking on the box labeled "Refresh Graphs." This Web site also provides the feature of comparing a stock to several other stocks and indexes.

As you gain experience in technical analysis, you may want more depth and variety in the information available to you. This Web site provides several other more complex types of charts for you to review. And when you know the kind of technical information you want, it allows you to customize your own charts with a service called, "Interactive Graph."

## STOCKCHARTS.COM WEB SITE

This Web site provides a comprehensive review of thousands of charts of stocks and mutual funds. It also displays several charts on the various stock market indexes such as the Dow Jones Industrial Index (Search symbol: $INDU).

It is important to be aware of the status of the overall market in addition to monitoring your individual investments. This site provides a means for getting this information and for making a technical analysis of market averages. Here is the procedure to follow:

- Enter www.stockcharts.com in the search slot of your home page or service provider.
- Click on the down arrowhead next to "Sharp Chart."

- Select "Gallery View."
- Enter "$INDU" in the search slot on the right-hand side of the screen.
- Click on "GO."

The screen that comes up provides a 6-month view of the Dow Jones Industrial Average. Scroll down to get a 3-year view of this average. From the resulting chart, you can interpret the current condition of the stock market: bullish, topping out, bearish, bottoming out, or range bound. Based on your opinion of the market situation, you could decide whether you want to adjust your portfolio more toward any style: conservative, balanced, or aggressive.

## BIG CHARTS WEB SITE

Another helpful and mostly free Web site is Big Charts at Web address www.bigcharts.com. This site also displays thousands of stock charts and provides a customization service called, "Interactive Charting." Here is the procedure for using this service:

- Enter the Web address in the search slot of your service provider or your home page.
- At the Web site, enter a stock symbol in the search slot.
- Click on "Interactive Charting."
- A separate window appears at the left side of the screen.
- Scroll down that window and three options appear.
- Select "Indicators."
- Scroll the window down again and several selections appear, including "Lower Indicators."
- Click on that one and a roll-up list appears giving you a choice of several indicators.
- Click on "Money Flow."
- Scroll back up to the top of the window and click on "Draw Chart."

A chart of the stock price appears in the right side of the screen. At the bottom of the chart, a line representing the flow of money into or out of the stock appears. It is designed to fluctuate above and below the centerline, which is neutral, and is given the designation of zero. If the money line is above zero, it indicates a flow of money into the stock. If the line is below zero, it indicates a flow of money out of the stock.

Following the procedure outlined above, 20 additional technical indicators are available at your request. And this site has many other informative features for you to explore.

These and other Web sites are described in Appendix C.

## APPLICATION EXERCISES

### Section 1

Go to the Yahoo! Finance Web site www.finance.yahoo.com. Repeat the following steps several times:

- Enter a stock symbol of your choice.
- Click "Go."
- When the first screen appears click on "Technical Analysis" in the left column.
- Click on 200 day EMA.
- Scroll down to see chart.
- Check the relationship between the stock price and the moving average.
- Look for two positive signs and two negative signs.
- As you find each sign, make a brief note as to what it is.
- Look at the next page to see the two positive and two negative signs.

**Positive Signs**

- Stock price has moved above the moving average.
- Moving average is following stock price upward.

**Negative Signs**

- Stock price has moved below the moving average.
- Moving average is following stock price downward.

## *Section 2*

- Go to the Clear Station Web site www.clearstation.com.
- Locate the A-List on the screen.
- Copy the symbols of the stocks at the top of the list that have "Record Price Breakouts."
- Close this Web site and go to the Yahoo! Finance Web site www.finance.yahoo.com.
- After entering each symbol in the search slot, repeat these steps several times.
- Click "Go."
- Click "Technical Analysis."
- Click 50- and 200-day EMAs.
- Check relationships between stock price and the two moving averages.
- Look for three positive signs.
- Make notes as to what they are.
- Look at the next page to see them.

## Three Positive Signs

- Stock price moves above the long moving average.
- Short moving average moves above long moving average.
- Stock price and short moving average move above long moving average.

# 7

# ANALYZING CLOSED-END FUNDS

## INTRODUCTION

When a closed-end fund (CEF) is established, a limited number of shares are issued, and the fund is traded on the market like a stock. To buy a closed-end fund, you can place a limit order at the price you are willing to pay and you can buy any amount of shares. When buying an open-ended mutual fund you cannot specify the price you want to pay. You must accept the price as determined by fund management as of the close of business. And you must invest a minimum amount of money as specified by each fund's rules. Closed-end funds are popular with investors because many of them pay higher dividends than most stocks and open-ended mutual funds, and you can buy or sell them any time the market is open.

The managers of closed-end funds invest in a wide variety of assets, including common and preferred stocks, United States government bonds and notes, foreign bonds and notes, domestic and foreign corporate bonds, municipal bonds, real estate investment trusts, and other financial instruments. Because of this broad diversification, these funds have lower risk than many individual stocks and nondiversified mutual funds.

Their dividends are more reliable because the cash flow into these funds comes from many different sources. A few of these funds pay dividends monthly and are so confident of their revenue stream that they declare the dividends for three months in advance, instead of one month at a time.

Most of these funds are managed by well-respected investment banks whose fund managers are experienced in both domestic and international investments. Their ability to find investment opportunities on a global basis gives them a competitive advantage when compared to funds that take a more provincial approach to investing. This flexible, worldwide approach allows for a higher return on their investments, which is passed on to shareholders in the form of high dividends.

## CLOSED-END FUND ANALYSIS

An important aspect of investigating a closed-end fund is assessing the relationship between the price of the fund and its net asset value (NAV). (*Net asset value* is the total value of the assets in the fund's portfolio minus the total amount of the fund's liabilities, divided by the number of outstanding shares.) *Barron's* magazine and other financial publications show price quotes on the funds together with data on the funds' net asset values. In many cases, the prices of the funds' shares are below the net asset values, and in these instances the shares of the funds can be bought at a discount.

In the following series of illustrations, a variety of relationships between closed-end fund prices and their net asset values will be illustrated. The analytical methods used in the following section of this chapter are most helpful when there are wide differences between the market price and the net asset value. However, as will be shown, even when the differences are small, an alert investor can still find profit opportunities in those discrepancies.

Refer to Chart 7-1. Here we see a closed-end fund price in a very narrow trading range. This fund has been selling at a discount

## CHART 7-1

Buy and Hold Closed-End Fund for Income

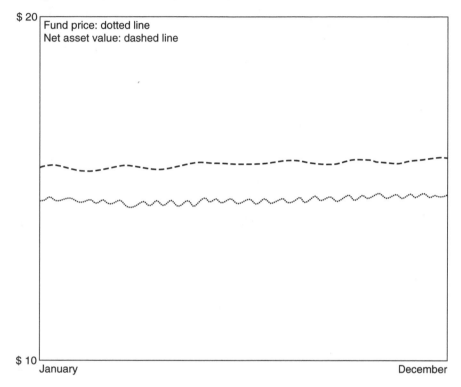

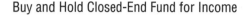

from its net asset value. Much of the time there are about as many funds selling at a discount as there are selling at a premium. The size of the discounts can range up to 20 percent, and the size of the premiums can range up to 40 percent. This fund pays a high dividend, which is the main reason an investor would want it as a part of a balanced portfolio.

Refer to Chart 7-2. In this case, both the price of the closed-end fund and its net asset value are in well-defined uptrends. This fund also pays a high dividend. As long as the net asset value rises along with the price of the fund, there is good reason to hold on to it. When the net asset value of a fund rises steadily, it is evidence the fund is being well managed and that is why

**CHART 7-2**

Buy Closed-End Fund for Income and Capital Gain

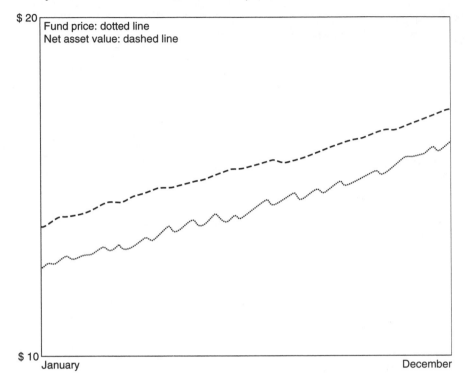

Fund price: dotted line
Net asset value: dashed line

$ 20

$ 10

January                                                                    December

investors are bidding the price up. If an investor sells the fund, he or she will have received a high income flow plus a sizeable capital gain.

Refer to Chart 7-3. In this case, the price of the closed-end fund drops below its net asset value for a while. In this time period, the fund can be bought at a discount for its high dividend. If the price of the fund and the net asset value remain stable, the investor has no capital gain but does benefit from the high income flow.

Refer to Chart 7-4. Here the price of the closed-end fund is well above its net asset value. Apparently some investors believe the fund is worth more than its net asset value and are willing to pay the premium price. If the dividend is significantly higher than

## CHART 7-3

Buy and Hold Closed-End Fund for Income

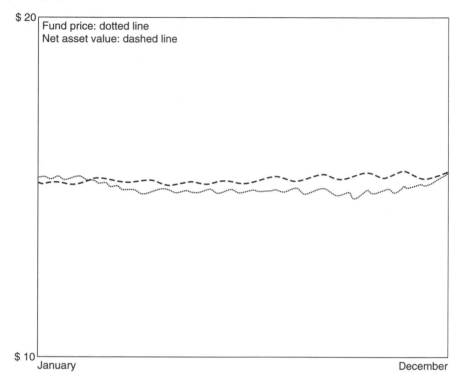

$ 20

Fund price: dotted line
Net asset value: dashed line

$ 10
January                                                                   December

the dividends available from other closed-end funds, the premium price may be justified. On the other hand, if there is little or no difference in the dividend levels, investing at a discount is preferable to paying a premium price for a fund.

Refer to Chart 7-5. In some instances, the market price of a closed-end fund makes a steep uptrend while the net asset value remains relatively unchanged. This situation may develop when a fund gets positive publicity on television or in financial publications. This very high premium of market price over net asset value raises the question of overpricing. Market price premiums up to 20 percent can be justified for several reasons. The management of the fund may have a good track record; the fund may be recommended

## CHART 7-4

Don't Buy Closed-End Fund at Premium Price

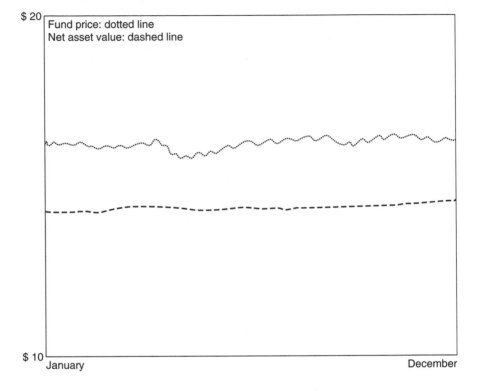

by a respected analyst; or the fund may be heavily invested in fast-growing countries. But if the differential between the fund price and the net asset value widens further, it is difficult to justify premium prices of more than 20 percent.

An investor having a large paper profit in such a fund should consider the risk. When the price of a fund is far beyond the net asset value, an analyst may downgrade the fund on the basis of its being overpriced. If this happens, the price would be subject to a quick drop and the investor could lose much or all of the paper profit.

Chart 7-6 illustrates the ideal closed-end fund from the perspective of a buy and hold investor. This investor purchased at a discount from the net asset value. During the following year, the market price of the fund rose to a level of about a 20 percent premium above the net asset value. The price of the fund then remained there. With the high dividend and a sizeable paper profit, the investor has an ideal long-term holding for a balanced portfolio.

**CHART 7-5**

Closed-End Fund at Excessive Price

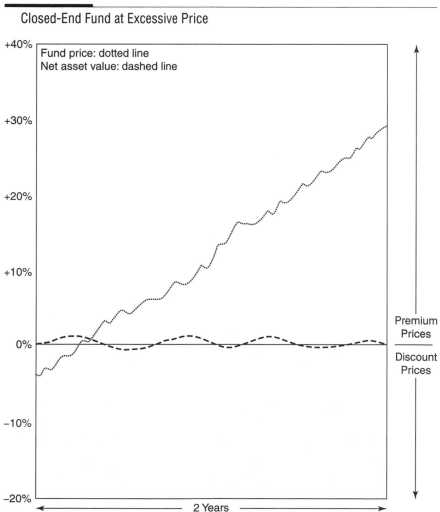

## CHART 7-6

Ideal Closed-End Fund to Buy and Hold

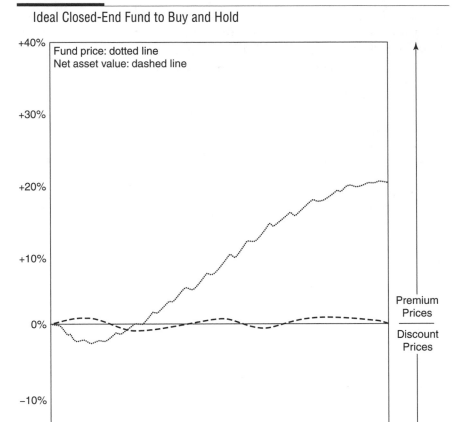

## GUIDELINES FOR TRADING CLOSED-END FUNDS

Here are some suggestions for buying, holding, and selling closed-end funds.

- Buy a fund that is discounted at no more than 10 percent. A fund selling at a discount larger than 10 percent is viewed by other investors with skepticism. It's possible the fund has poor management and/or there are concerns about the way some of the assets have been evaluated. (The evaluation of a fund's assets is not always done with complete accuracy.) But whatever the cause, the low price indicates many investors have serious doubts about the prospects for the fund.

- Hold a fund during a rise up to a 20 percent premium. Beyond that level the fund is becoming overpriced in relation to the value of its assets and the risk in holding it is rising steadily with the price. If the fund price rises toward a 30 percent premium, continue to hold only if you are willing and able to handle a high-risk situation.

- Sell if the price rises above a 30 percent premium. This is an excessive valuation and a high-risk situation. Any negative event or opinion expressed by a commentator or an analyst could make the price drop quickly.

## CLOSED-END FUND ASSOCIATION WEB SITE

To get a more detailed look at closed-end funds, it's worthwhile to explore a Web site that is devoted to closed-end funds. This site is sponsored by the Closed-End Fund Association. The Web address is www.cefa.com.

When you have access to a computer and some spare time, you can take a tour of this site, which has many educational features. Start by putting the site address in the search slot of your service provider or home page. At the home page of the Closed-End Fund Association look at the right-hand side of the screen and scroll down through the following topics: "Today's Leaders," "Tools," "Education Center," and "Free Booklets."

To be an informed investor, you can go into the Education Center and read the information presented under the topics of "Overview," "Advantages," "Investment Risks," and "Types of CEFs." After reading these introductory descriptions, check the closed-end fund listings in *Barron's* weekly magazine. This listing shows the name and symbol for each fund along with its market price, premium over or discount from the net asset value, and the past year's yield for the fund. Some of the types of funds listed are: World Equity, World Income, Investment Grade Bonds, and National Muni Bonds. After you decide which categories are of most interest to you, write down the names of several funds and their symbols. You will then be ready to start researching these funds.

In the upper left-hand corner of the Closed-End Fund Association Web site home page is a search slot labeled "Ticker/Keyboard." Enter a fund symbol in this slot and see a display showing the net asset value, market price, premium above or discount below the market price, and yields for various time periods. Below this display is a statement, "Click here for more information on this fund." Click on that statement. You then see additional information that includes a description of the fund objectives, the top 10 holdings in the fund, the top 10 industries or sectors in the fund, and the percentage of the fund's assets invested in each industry or sector as of the end of the preceding quarter. After reading this detailed information, you have a general idea of the composition of that fund.

Now let's review the suitability of these various types of funds for each of the three portfolio styles described in Chapter 5. None of these funds would be appropriate for an aggressive portfolio because they are not aimed at achieving large capital gains. Several of the fund types could be suitable for a balanced portfolio because of their high income flow objectives. These are the World Equity, World Income, and National Muni Bond funds. Regarding the conservative portfolio, only an investment grade bond fund would be suitable, if it could be bought at a discount from its net asset value.

## APPLICATION EXERCISE

### Section 1

When you have some time available, check the list of World Income funds in the closed-end funds section of *Barron's* magazine and select three with a high 12-months' yield that are selling at a discount from net asset value. Copy the names of the funds and symbols. Then go to the www.cefa.com site and enter one symbol. Review the display of data to verify the discount and the market return for one year. Then click on "Click here for more information on this fund." Make notes on the major holdings in the fund. Repeat this procedure for each of the other two symbols. When you are done, compare the three funds and decide which one, if any, could be appropriate for your portfolio.

## Section 2

Check the list of funds under the heading of World Equity funds in the closed-end funds section of *Barron's* magazine. Look for the highest-yielding funds selling at a discount from net asset value. Copy the names and symbols for three funds. Then go to the Closed-End Fund Association Web site and repeat the evaluation process described in Section 1.

## Section 3

Repeat the evaluation process for three funds in the category of National Muni funds.

## Section 4

Repeat the evaluation process for three funds in the category of Investment Grade Bonds.


When you have finished the four sections of this exercise you should have an informed opinion as to whether closed-end funds are an appropriate investment for you.

## REVIEW EXERCISE

This review exercise will help you to verify that you have learned how to analyze closed-end funds whose prices vary from their net asset value.

1. Refer to Chart 7-7. The net asset value of this fund has been rising steadily and the price of the fund has been rising with it. The fund pays a high dividend, and a holder of this fund can also make a capital gain on the investment.

For which type of portfolio would this fund be most appropriate: aggressive, balanced, or conservative?

### CHART 7-7

Question 1

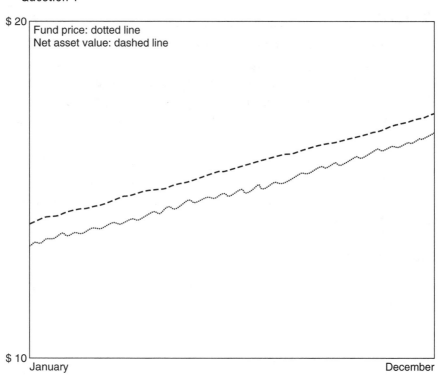

Fund price: dotted line
Net asset value: dashed line

$ 20

$ 10

January                                        December

## *Answer to Question 1*

This fund would be most suitable for a balanced fund because it meets both objectives of income flow and capital gains.

2. Refer to Chart 7-8. Here the fund is selling at a premium over the net asset value of the fund. The fund is paying a dividend similar to those paid by other closed-end funds. All other things being equal, if an investor has a choice of buying this fund at a premium price or another fund of the same type at a discount, which purchase would be more prudent from a monetary perspective?

**CHART 7-8**

Question 2

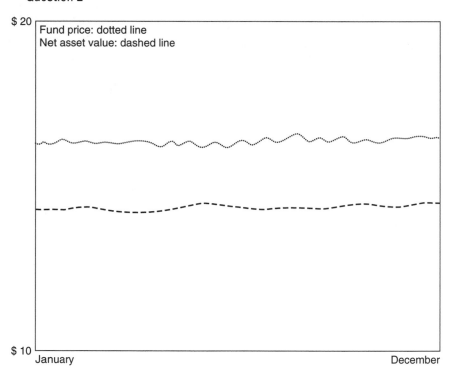

## Answer to Question 2

Buying the same type of fund at a discount would be the prudent action. Buying a fund at a premium price usually means you are not getting the best value for your money. When you buy a fund at a discount, you are often getting a bargain.

3. Refer to Chart 7-9. The latest price of this fund is about 30 percent higher than its net asset value. What is the level of risk in this situation: low, medium, or high?

**CHART 7-9**

Question 3

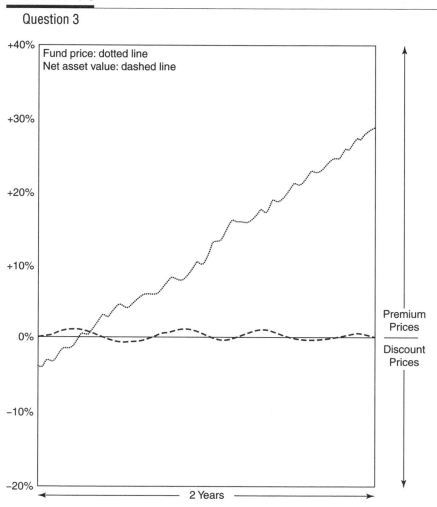

## *Answer to Question 3*

The level of risk in this situation is very high. Since the fund is over-priced by 30 percent, the main danger is that someone with access to the financial media will state a reason for why the fund's high price is not justified. No matter what reason is given, just describing the fund as being overpriced would probably set off a large decline in the fund. To avoid getting caught in this type of situation, the sensible thing to do is to sell the fund while you have a sizeable capital gain.

# 8

# ANALYZING PREFERRED STOCKS

## INTRODUCTION

Preferred stocks have several advantages over common stocks. They are less risky because the issuer promises to return par value when the stock is called. They are often issued with a dividend higher than the common stock dividend so they serve the dual purpose of producing income while preserving capital. And the preferred stock dividend must be paid before any payment can be made on the common stock.

You have probably been aware of these characteristics, but you may not know there are substantial profits to be made by purchasing preferred stocks at a discount and selling them at a premium price.

This type of transaction is possible because the prices of some preferred stocks fluctuate above and below the issue price, which in many cases is $25. The prices usually fluctuate within $2 of the issue price. Here's an example of how profitable it can be when you buy at a discount and sell at a premium.

Suppose you purchase a $25 par value stock for $23.50, hold it a year while collecting a dividend of 6 percent, and sell it for $26.50. At the conclusion of that round-trip transaction, you would have collected 6 percent in dividends and 12 percent in capital gains, which totals to a profit of 18 percent in one year.

You can find listings of preferred stocks in the *Wall Street Journal*, *Barron's* weekly magazine, and *Investor's Business Daily*. *Barron's* shows the current price, yield, and the new highs and lows for the year. By checking through the list you should be able to find a few stocks priced at a discount large enough to deliver a profit from either rising to a premium price or being called at par value.

## SELECTING PREFERRED STOCKS

By using technical analysis, you will be able to select a particular stock that has a good chance of rising above the par value of $25. So you will eventually get the capital gain in addition to the dividend. Here are two Web sites where you can get price and volume charts on both the preferred and common stocks of many companies: www.clearstation.com and www.finance.yahoo.com.

Once you have identified preferred stocks that look promising, you can get all the important information on any preferred issue at the Web site, www.quantumonline.com. This site shows the date of issue, the issue price, the call date, the liquidation value (amount to be paid for each share when the stock is called), and other pertinent details.

When researching these information sources, look for stocks with the following attributes:

- The call date should be at least three years later than the current date.

- The current stock price should be at a discount from par value of at least $1.

- Both the common stock and preferred stocks should have positive patterns or formations such as an uptrend, an ascending triangle, a bottoming formation, or an upside breakout from a trading range.

- To increase the likelihood of selling the stock at a favorable price, the average daily trading volume should be at least 10,000 shares.

If you can buy a stock meeting those criteria, you can collect the dividend for at least a year and make at least $1 profit per share when the stock is called. If the stock price rises above par value before it is called, you will have the opportunity to make a larger profit prior to the call date.

## TRADING PREFERRED STOCKS

The following series of charts illustrates some methods of trading preferred stocks for capital gains over and above the dividend income that each stock provides.

Refer to Chart 8-1. This chart presents the ideal price pattern from an investor's perspective. The price declines early in the five-year life of the stock. This allows a purchase at a discount from par

### CHART 8-1

Preferred Stock Produces Large Net Profit

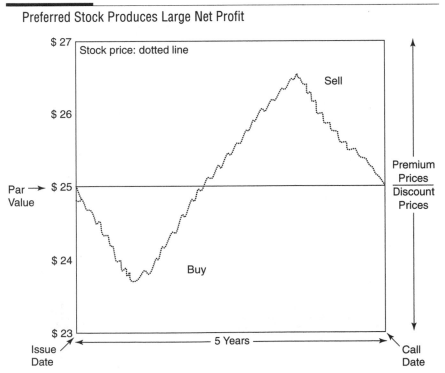

value. The price then rises to a large premium where it can be sold for a profit. When the dividends are added to the capital gain, the investor has a large net profit.

Refer to Chart 8-2. Here is another price pattern from which an investor can profit. This investor buys the stock at a large discount with the intention of selling it at a premium price. In this case the premium price does not materialize, but a profit can still be made by waiting for the call date. When the stock is called, the investor makes a smaller capital gain than hoped for, but when added to the dividends, still has a sizeable profit.

Refer to Chart 8-3. Here is another price formation from which an investor can profit. The investor buys the stock at a small discount. In this case the price does what the investor wants it to by rising to a large premium. At that level the investor realizes it's bet-

## CHART 8-2

Hold Preferred Stock to Call Date

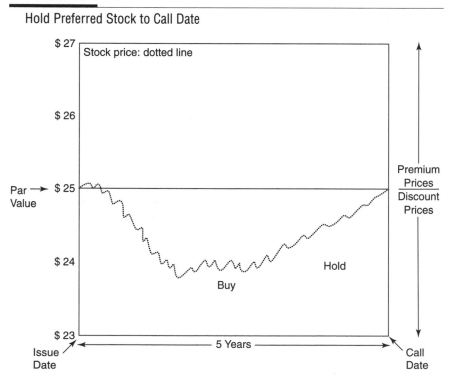

## CHART 8-3

Sell Preferred Stock before Call Date

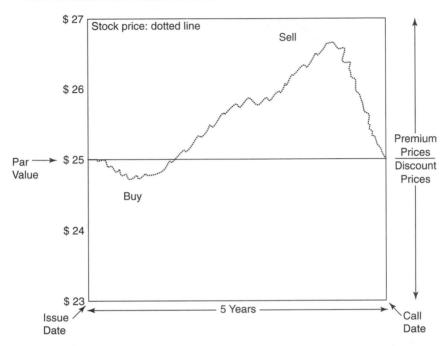

ter not to wait for the stock to be called. The investor then sells for a premium price. Adding the capital gains to a couple of years of dividends results in a significant net profit.

Refer to Chart 8-4. This chart displays a flat line formation that eliminates the possibility of a capital gain. Investors agree that the stock is priced correctly, and it trades near its par value plus or minus a few cents. If this stock were paying a high dividend, an investor could buy it for income. But without that incentive, there's no reason to buy this stock. It would be a waste of time.

Refer to Chart 8-5. This chart shows a typical price formation for the stock of a company that is paying a dividend on its common stock and has the highest rating on its bonds. It pays a smaller than average dividend on this preferred stock, which is why it trades at a small premium. Since the stock price fluctuates in a range close to par value, there's no reason to buy it for a capital gain. However, as

## CHART 8-4

Preferred Stock Flat Line Formation

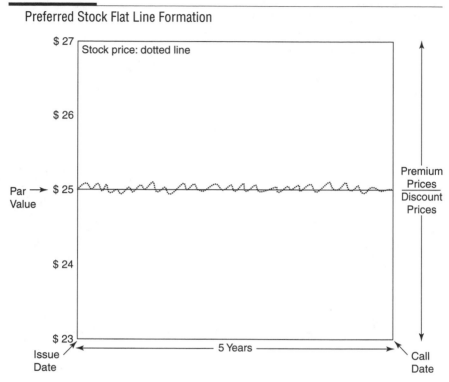

a means of preserving capital, this type of preferred stock is an appropriate investment in a bear market when many common stocks would be declining in value.

Refer to Chart 8-6. A short while after this preferred stock was issued, the company's profits started to decline. A little later, the company began to report increasing losses. The common and preferred stocks went into steep downtrends. Eventually the company eliminated the common stock dividend and suspended the preferred stock dividend. If this were a cumulative preferred stock, the stockholders could hope to get the missed dividend payments when the company could afford to pay them. They could also hope to receive payment of par value for the preferred stock when the company calls it. This situation illustrates the risk of owning the preferred stock in a company that cannot maintain its profitability.

## CHART 8-5

Preferred Stock Preserves Capital

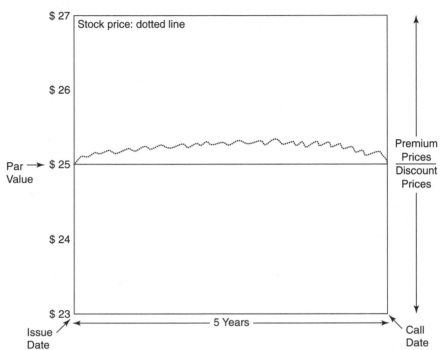

**CHART 8-6**

High-Risk Preferred Stock

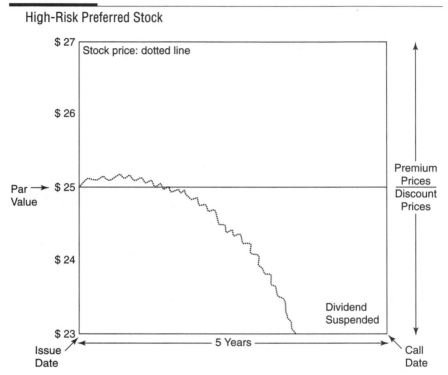

## REVIEW EXERCISE

This review exercise will help you determine how well you have learned the methods of trading preferred stocks. Your objective in this exercise is to distinguish between price formations that allow for a capital gain and those that do not. The correct answer to each question appears on the page following each chart.

1. Refer to Chart 8-7. The dividend paid by this preferred stock is average compared to the dividends being paid by other preferred stocks at the current time. The company is in an industry that is not growing and its share of the market has remained stable for several years. Is this a situation that can produce a capital gain?

## CHART 8-7

Question 1

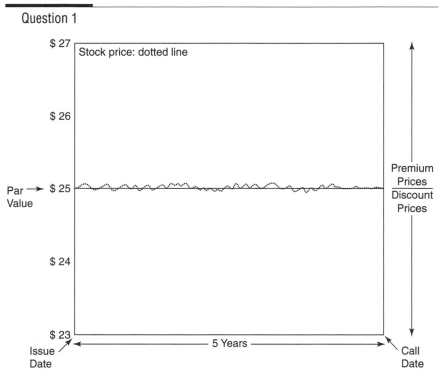

## Answer to Question 1

No. This type of price formation reflects a situation in which the prospects for the company are not positive. Unless there is a change for the better, this stock is not likely to move up enough to allow for a capital gain.

2. Refer to Chart 8-8. After a brief decline, this preferred stock traded at premium prices until it was called. The dividend paid by this stock was average compared to the dividends being paid by other companies. The reason for the rise in the stock price was that the company began to be more profitable a brief time after the stock was issued. Can a profit be made from buying and selling a stock with a price pattern like this?

### CHART 8-8

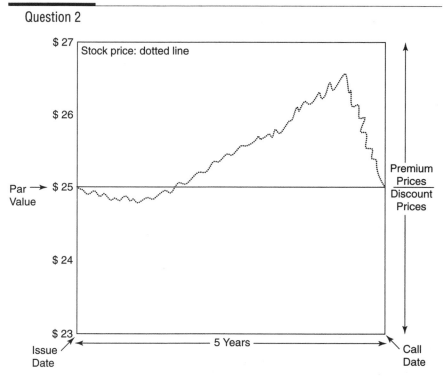

Question 2

## *Answer to Question 2*

Yes. A profit can be made from buying and selling a stock with this type of pattern. Before the money gained from this stock issue was put to work, the price declined slightly. As the company used the money to improve its profitability, the price of the stock rose and provided the opportunity for an investor to make a capital gain. When the dividends received are added to the gain, the net profit is sizeable.

3. Refer to Chart 8-9. The price of this preferred stock never went above its par value. The company wanted to use the money gained from the issue of this stock to buy out a small competitor. But the target company accepted a buyout offer from another company in the industry. Some of the preferred stockholders decided to sell on this news, driving the price of the stock down for more than a year. The company managed to maintain its profitability despite the rejection of its offer. The company paid the dividends for five years and then called the stock and paid stockholders par value. Can a capital gain be made from a transaction on a stock with this type of price pattern?

## CHART 8-9

Question 3

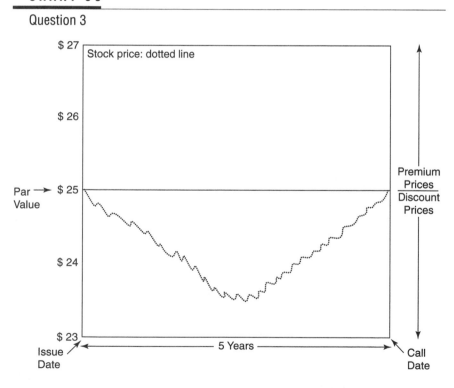

## *Answer to Question 3*

Yes. A capital gain can be made on a preferred stock with a price pattern like this. Although the market price remains below par value, when it goes below $24 per share, it is selling at a large discount. An investor who sees the uptrend starting can purchase the stock and wait for the call date to receive par value and make a capital gain of approximately 5 percent, in addition to the dividends received previously.

4. Refer to Chart 8-10. This type of price formation can be found in preferred stocks that pay a small dividend. Some investors buy these stocks because the issuing company has a reputation for sound business practices and can be relied on to pay the dividend through variations in economic conditions. Can a capital gain be made by buying and selling a stock with a price pattern like this?

## CHART 8-10

Question 4

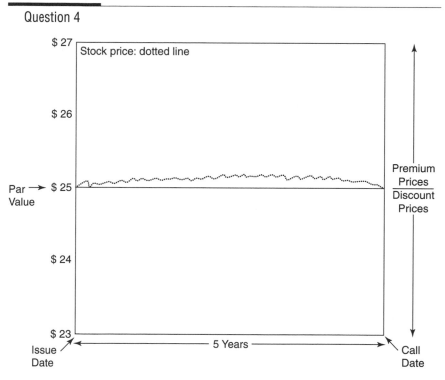

## *Answer to Question 4*

No. A capital gain cannot be made on a stock with a price pattern like this. There is not enough price fluctuation to allow for any capital gain, and an investor buying this stock after it is issued will have a small capital loss when it is called.

5. Refer to Chart 8-11. This stock paid a dividend higher than those being paid by most other preferred stocks being issued at the time. The high dividend kept investors buying the stock for a while. But then the stock price went into a steep downtrend when operating losses were reported. Can a capital gain be made from buying and selling a stock with a price pattern like this?

## CHART 8-11

Question 5

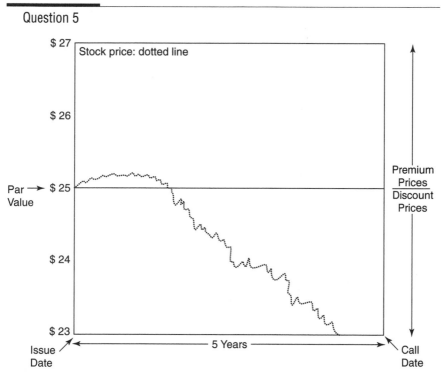

## *Answer to Question 5*

Not likely. This is a very high-risk situation. After the price goes into a downtrend because of poor performance, the chance for a capital gain becomes very remote. The company might suspend the dividend and the investor could only get the dividends later if it is cumulative. In addition, the company might be unable to redeem the stock on the call date and delay the redemption for a long time.

# 9

# ANALYZING REAL ESTATE INVESTMENT TRUSTS (REITs)

## INTRODUCTION

Real Estate Investment Trusts (REITs) provide an opportunity to make investments that pay high dividends and also have the potential to produce capital gains. REITs are required to pay out 90 percent of their earnings to their stockholders. This feature makes them very popular with investors who are seeking high income flow. And when real estate values are rising, these investments have great appeal to those who are looking for a balance of income flow and capital gains.

## CHARACTERISTICS OF REITs

The two main types of REITs are those that deal in mortgage-backed securities and those that own real properties and whose earnings are based primarily on rental income. Both types of REITs can be very profitable, but the earnings of those dealing in mortgage-backed securities are volatile because they are largely dependent on short-term interest rates being lower than long-term interest rates. (Companies dealing in mortgage-backed securities borrow money at low short-term rates and lend money at higher long-term rates. Consequently, their profit margins are dependent on the spread between these rates.) The REITs based on mortgage-backed securities are mostly suitable for investors who are willing to accept the fluctuating dividend payouts due to changes in the short- and long-term interest rates.

## REITs HOLDING REAL PROPERTIES

REITs that own real properties have easily understood business models based on collecting rents from their lessees. Some of these REITs write leases that last for 10 years, which makes the rental income flow more reliable. REITs may own health care facilities, regional malls, neighborhood shopping centers, office buildings, apartment complexes, industrial parks, restaurant chains, self-storage facilities, amusement parks, assisted living facilities, or hotels and other types of income-producing properties.

REIT funds usually own 40 or more REITs from the several types of real properties mentioned above. This diversification results in a lower risk level for the investor than owning one REIT because their profits come from a large group of real estate investments. Like individual REITs, REIT funds are required to pay 90 percent of their profits to their stockholders.

If you don't own any real estate and you wish to broaden your investments beyond bonds and stock, you may want to consider adding a REIT or a REIT fund to diversify your portfolio. This would increase the income flow and add the potential of price appreciation that has characterized the real estate market in many sections of the country. The best time to buy a REIT or a REIT fund is when long-term interest rates are high.

## APPLICATION EXERCISE

Here is an exercise to familiarize you with the kind of information on REITs available on the Internet.

Go to the National Association of REITs' Web site at www. investinREITs.com. Click on "Closed-End Funds." A list of REIT funds and their stock market symbols is presented. Select a symbol and click on it. The Yahoo! Financial screen appears and shows basic information on the REIT fund you selected. One of the important items shown is the dollar amount of the dividend for a year and the percentage yield of that dividend.

At the left side of the screen click on "Technical Analysis." You can then analyze the stock price pattern by looking for positive features and making note of them. Then return to the National Association of REITs home page and repeat this procedure for several REIT funds. After comparing the different REIT funds, you can decide if you want to include any of these funds in your portfolio.

If you have detailed knowledge of the real estate business and have reason to believe that a particular type of real estate has promising long-term prospects, you may want to research individual REITs. To do this, go back to the National Association of REITs' Web site and this time click on "REITs by Ticker Symbol." A list of hundreds of REITs is presented and you can investigate as many as you like using the Yahoo! Finance Web site as you did for the REIT funds.

# FINAL REVIEW EXERCISE

This exercise gives you an opportunity to measure how well you have learned the basic concepts of technical analysis. There are a total of 25 problems regarding the price and moving average patterns you have seen. Question 1 provides 15 of these problems. After answering each question, go to the next page to see the correct answer. Each of the 25 problems is worth 4 percentage points.

1. On the next page, 15 stock price patterns are shown. Beneath the stock price patterns are the names of these patterns. Each pattern has a number assigned to it. Identify each price pattern and place the assigned number in the box with the pattern. Then check your 15 answers on the following page. Each correct answer is worth 4 percentage points.

## FINAL REVIEW

### Question 1

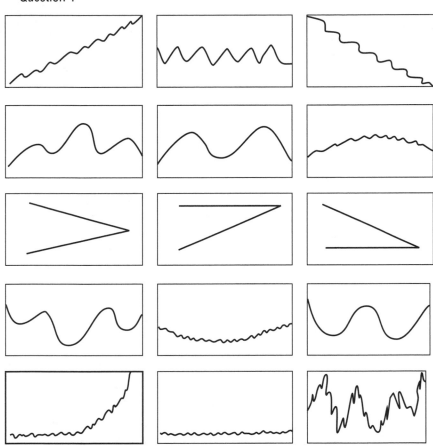

| | |
|---|---|
| 1. Ascending Triangle | 8. Uptrend |
| 2. Double Bottom | 9. Head and Shoulders |
| 3. Flat Line Formation | 10. Trading Range |
| 4. Descending Triangle | 11. Downtrend |
| 5. Rounding Bottom | 12. Double Top |
| 6. Parabolic Curve | 13. Symmetrical Triangle |
| 7. Inverted Head and Shoulders | 14. Rounding Top |
| | 15. Erratic Volatility |

## FINAL REVIEW

Answers to Question 1

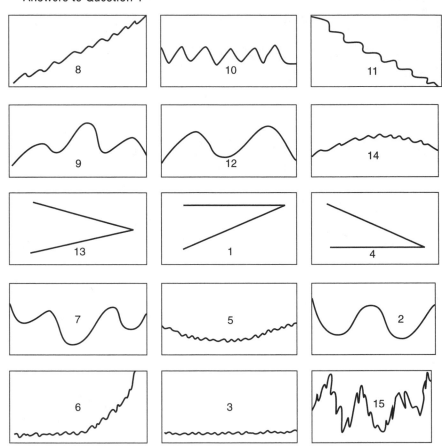

1. Ascending Triangle
2. Double Bottom
3. Flat Line Formation
4. Descending Triangle
5. Rounding Bottom
6. Parabolic Curve
7. Inverted Head and Shoulders

8. Uptrend
9. Head and Shoulders
10. Trading Range
11. Downtrend
12. Double Top
13. Symmetrical Triangle
14. Rounding Top
15. Erratic Volatility

2. In this breakout from a trading range, is the stock price likely to develop momentum to the upside?

**FINAL REVIEW**

Question 2

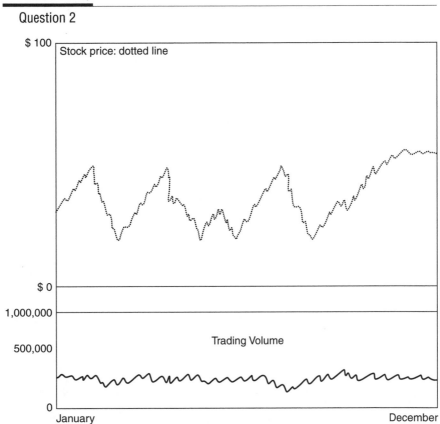

## Answer to Question 2

No. There was no increase in trading volume.

3. In this breakout from a symmetrical triangle, does the low volume imply the decline will not be large?

**FINAL REVIEW**

Question 3

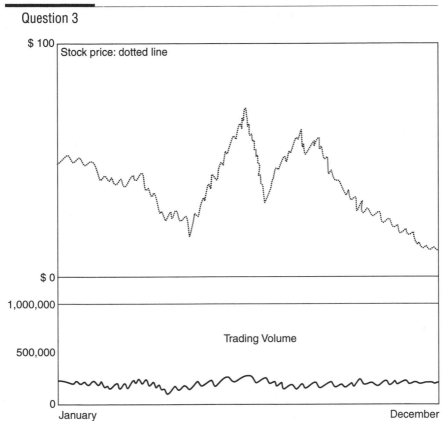

## Answer to Question 3

No. It does not take high trading volume to make a large decline from a breakout to the downside. All it takes is a scarcity of buyers compared to sellers, which creates a condition where the price can drift lower for an extended period.

4. This short-term average has crossed above the long-term average. Does the move have any implication for the price of the stock?

## FINAL REVIEW

### Question 4

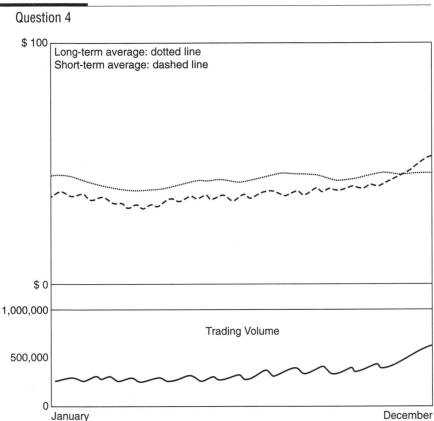

## *Answer to Question 4*

Yes. The short-term average reflects prices that are more up to date than those in the long-term average, and this crossing implies the price movement to the upside will continue for a while.

5. This moving average is trailing the upward move in the stock price. Does this relationship confirm the uptrend?

**FINAL REVIEW**

Question 5

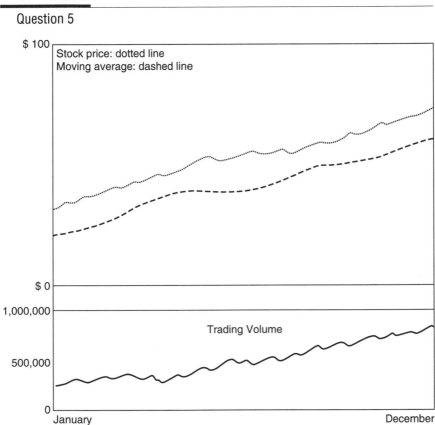

## *Answer to Question 5*

Yes. It confirms that the uptrend will continue until the price goes down through the moving average.

6. This stock price has crossed up through the moving average. Can this be interpreted as a buy signal?

Question 6

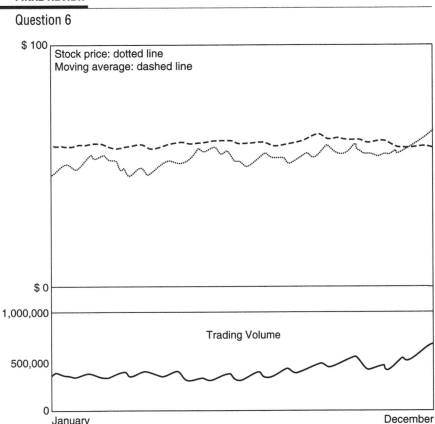

## Answer to Question 6

Yes. It is a buy signal, and the increasing trading volume validates it.

7. True or false? Since there are only two phases to a double bottom, it is likely to result in a smaller price gain than the three-phased inverted head and shoulders pattern.

**FINAL REVIEW**

Question 7

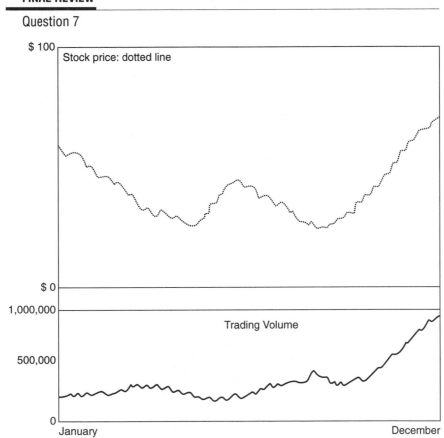

## Answer to Question 7

False. A double bottom pattern has the potential to produce a price gain equal to that produced by an inverted head and shoulders pattern. The amount of gain resulting from both patterns depends on the size of the pattern rather than the shape.

8. For which type of portfolio are these investments most suitable: aggressive, balanced, or conservative?

**FINAL REVIEW**

Question 8

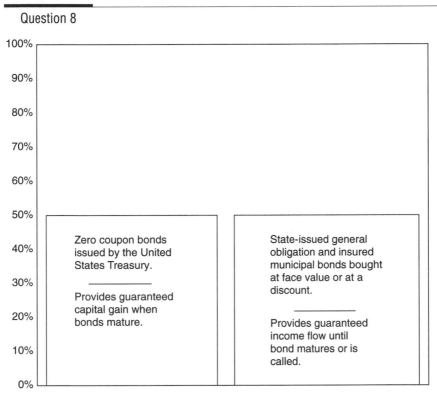

## *Answer to Question 8*

These investments are most suitable for a conservative portfolio because they are among the safest available.

9. Refer to the two stock price charts below. Given a choice, in which trading range would an active trader be likely to make the most profit?

## FINAL REVIEW

Question 9

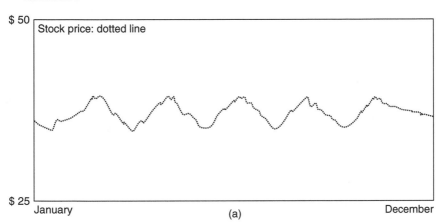

(a)

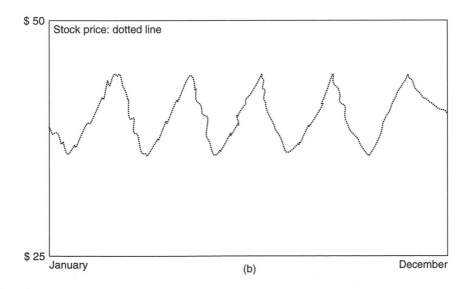

(b)

## *Answer to Question 9*

An active trader is likely to make more profit trading the stock in the bottom chart (b) because the price difference between the bottom and top of the range is larger.

10. Each investor now has a profit of $15. Referring to the two charts below, if both investors continue to hold their stock until the end of the next quarter, which investor is likely to have the larger profit at that point?

**FINAL REVIEW**

Question 10

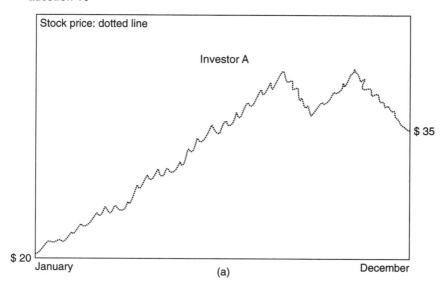

(a)

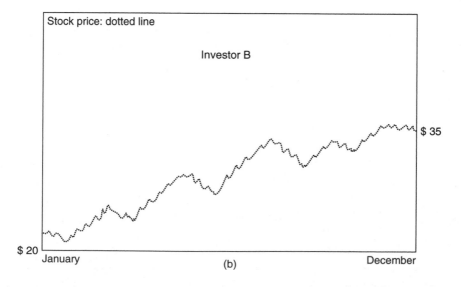

(b)

## Answer to Question 10

Investor B should have the larger profit because the stock is in an uptrend while the stock Investor A is holding has made a double top.

11. Here are two upside breakouts from ascending triangles. Which investor is likely to have a larger profit as a result of these breakouts?

**FINAL REVIEW**

Question 11

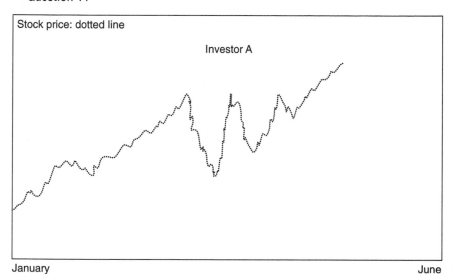

## *Answer to Question 11*

Investor A is likely to have more profit because the ascending triangle is larger.

# LIST OF ILLUSTRATIONS

# B

# GLOSSARY

Accumulation—Purchases of large quantities of stock by knowledgeable investors with strong finances who believe the shares have become greatly underpriced.

Ascending Triangle—A price pattern formed by two or more tops at the same level and two or more bottoms, with each successive bottom being higher than preceding bottom(s). A horizontal line drawn across the tops is met by the ascending line drawn across the bottoms, thus creating an upward-slanting wedge.

Bear Market—An extended time period during which stock averages trend lower, and any upward price moves are relatively short in duration.

Bottoming Out—A process by which an extended downtrend is converted into an uptrend. This change in direction can occur over a short, intermediate, or long period of time.

Breakout—*See Downside Breakout and Upside Breakout.*

Bull Market—An extended time period during which stock averages trend higher, and any downward price moves are relatively short in duration.

Buy Signal—The signal given when a breakout occurs to the upside.

Call Date—The date after which a preferred stock or a bond may be called by the issuer.

Call Price—The monetary amount to be returned to the investor when a preferred stock or a bond is called by the issuer.

Capital Gain—The amount of profit made on a completed transaction.

Capital Loss—The amount of loss taken on a completed transaction.

Closed-End Fund—A fund that issues a certain number of shares and never increases that amount. This type of fund trades on the market like a stock, and the price patterns are subject to technical analysis.

Common Stock—The basic form of ownership in a corporation that entitles the owner to the right to vote the shares and to a proportionate share of the common stock dividends.

Continuation Formation—The price pattern formed when the price direction of the stock is the same as it enters and exits the formation. The pattern serves as a rest area in the price movement—up or down. Continuation formations can be triangles, or trading ranges, or any other vertically limited form lasting a short or intermediate time period.

Demand—The total number of shares sought for purchase by all interested and capable parties.

Descending Triangle—The price pattern formed by two or more descending tops and two or more bottoms at the same level. A line drawn across the tops meets the line drawn across the bottoms to form a downward-slanting wedge.

Discount Price—The price paid by a purchaser who buys a preferred stock or bond at a price below the face value. This term also applies to the purchase of a closed-end fund at a price below its net asset value.

Distribution—The sale of a large quantity of shares by knowledgeable stockholders who believe the stock has become greatly overpriced.

Double Bottom—The price pattern formed when a stock price declines to a bottom, rises from that point, declines again to the same approximate price, and subsequently rises from that level beyond the preceding price rise.

Double Top—The price pattern formed when a stock price rises to a peak, drops from that point, rises again to the same approximate price, and subsequently falls from that level further than the previous drop.

Downside Breakout—A price drop through a support level or an uptrend line. This breakout event is normally followed by a price move to lower levels.

Downtrend Line—A line drawn through two or more descending tops.

Exponential Moving Average—An average price calculated from a consecutive series of prices with extra weight given to the more recent prices.

Fundamental Information—Details on company products, services, financial condition, competition, and any other factors affecting a company's financial results.

Globalization—The trend toward going beyond national borders to invest in companies, government bonds, and other international asset classes.

Issue Date—The date on which a security is issued to the public for purchase.

Intermediate Term—A period of time between one month and one year.

Liquidation Value—The price at which a security such as a preferred stock is to be redeemed when it is called or matures.

Long Term—A period of time one year or longer.

Moody's Bond Rating—A bond rating company that rates bonds from the highest (AAA) to the lowest (D).

Mortgage-Backed Securities—Individual mortgages assembled into packages (securitized) by some real estate investment trusts (REITs) and sold by them as investments to others in this business, who buy them for the income stream they deliver.

Net Asset Value per Share—The market value of the fund portfolio, minus any liabilities, divided by the number of shares in the fund.

Paper Loss—A loss that has not been taken, but remains on the books.

Paper Profit—A profit that has not been taken, but remains on the books.

Parabolic Curve—An increase in a stock price that accelerates until it is going almost straight up. This sharp rise cannot be sustained indefinitely, and after a while the most likely result is a swift decline to much lower levels.

Par Value—The stated value of a security when it is issued.

Preferred Stock—A class of stock that takes precedence over the common stock as to dividend payments.

Premium Price—The price paid by a purchaser who pays more than par value for a preferred stock or a bond. In the case of a closed-end fund, the purchaser pays more than the net asset value per share.

Range Bound—A term that refers to a stock market that lacks the momentum to move up or down for an extended period of time. In this condition, the market averages vacillate within a limited vertical distance.

Relative Strength—A rating of the price performance relative to other stocks. A rating of 75 indicates the performance of the stock is better than 75 percent of all other stocks. Any rating under 50 is a sign of weaker than average performance.

Resistance Level—The price level from which a stock has declined in its past attempt or attempts to penetrate it.

Rounding Bottom—The saucer-shaped curve that develops when a downtrend in a stock price gradually changes into an uptrend over a period of several weeks or longer.

Rounding Top—The upside-down saucer-shaped curve that develops when an uptrend in a stock price gradually changes into a downtrend over a period of several weeks or longer.

Sell Signal—The signal that is given when a breakout occurs to the downside.

Short Term—Any period of time that is one month or shorter.

Simple Moving Average—An average price calculated from a consecutive series of the most recent prices.

Standard & Poor's—A bond rating company that rates bonds from the highest investment grade to the lowest rating (from AAA to D).

Supply—The total number of shares available for sale from the holders of a stock.

Support Level—A price level from which a stock has risen after declining to it one or more times.

Symmetrical Triangle—A price pattern that develops when two or more consecutive descending tops are matched by two or more consecutive ascending bottoms. A straight line drawn across the tops and a straight line drawn across the bottoms meet to form a wedge-shaped figure with a horizontal orientation.

Topping Out—The process by which an extended uptrend is converted into a downtrend. This change in direction can be achieved in a short, intermediate, or long period of time.

Upside Breakout—A rise through a resistance level or a downtrend line. This breakout event is normally followed by a price move to higher levels if the breakout is accompanied by a large increase in trading volume.

Yield—The amount of return on a stock when dividends and profit or loss are added together. For bonds, it is the return on investment when interest and profit or loss are added together.

Zero Coupon Bond—A bond that pays no interest. The bond is bought at a discount, and the purchaser receives the face value of the bond at maturity. The amount of yield to the buyer is dependent on the size of the discount when the bond is purchased.

# C

# HELPFUL WEB SITES

On the following pages are descriptions of Internet Web sites. These sites were selected because they have a great deal of information, charts, diagrams, explanations, and definitions that can be helpful to technical analysts. Most of the content of the sites is offered without charge. Advanced services are also available to those who register with a site to become a member and pay the fee. You should become familiar with these sites to find out how they can provide you with the specific information necessary to help you make wise investment decisions.

The sites to be reviewed are listed below.

| Web Site Name | Web Site Address |
|---|---|
| Yahoo! Finance | www.Finance.Yahoo.com |
| Clear Station | www.ClearStation.com |
| StockCharts.com | www.Stockcharts.com |
| Big Charts | www.Bigcharts.com |
| Quantum On Line | www.QuantumOnLine.com |
| National Association of REITs | www.investinREITs.com |

## YAHOO! FINANCE WEB SITE

This site is well organized, comprehensive, and a good starting point for investigating both the technical and fundamental details on any company or mutual fund listed on the stock exchanges. It provides charts on thousands of stocks and funds that can be customized to provide the information you want. The charts can show different time periods from 1 day to 5 years, different length simple and exponential moving averages from 5 to 200 days, comparisons of the price performance of a subject stock or fund to up to four other stocks or funds and to three major stock market averages. It also gives information on insider trades, dividends, and details on the company's financial condition.

## CLEAR STATION WEB SITE

This Web site also contains thousands of charts. For each stock you can view a standard chart called, "Quote & 3-Point View." This chart shows the price range for 1 year, moving averages of 13 and 50 days' length, and the trading volume. Another display shows the Moving Average Convergence/Divergence (MACD) indicator, which highlights interacting trendlines that fluctuate above and below a horizontal line marking a neutral status. This display has indicators to pinpoint the times when the trendlines turn positive or negative. A third display is called the MACD Histogram. This is a series of vertical bars of different lengths that rise and fall to confirm the direction of the MACD trendlines. (By clicking on "MACD" next to the chart, detailed explanations of the MACD trendlines and the MACD Histogram are presented.) A fourth display shows two interacting trendlines that indicate whether a stock is overbought or oversold.

This site also provides a customization service called "Interactive Graph Tool." With it, you can customize charts with several technical indicators, three exponential moving averages, and time periods from 1 day to 10 years. Also available are news articles and fundamental information on the company.

## STOCKCHARTS.COM WEB SITE

This Web site provides a chart called "Sharp Chart" that shows the 50- and 200-day moving averages, the trading volume, the Relative Strength Indicator (RSI) for each stock, and the Moving Average

Convergence/Divergence indicator. During trading hours the chart can be updated to show the latest price.

Additional charts are shown under the heading of "Gallery View." This presentation shows three charts. The first chart is a 6-month chart with an indicator that shows whether money is flowing into or out of the stock. The second chart is a 2-year chart with a 200-day moving average. This longer time frame allows the investor to appreciate the larger perspective of the stock price trends and patterns. The last chart uses the Point and Figure charting style to identify uptrends and downtrends. These Point and Figure charts have the unique feature of specifying a price objective that is above or below the current price.

Another unique feature of this Web site is called "Chart School." This option is available on the home page. The chart school covers four topics in comprehensive fashion; chart analysis, indicator analysis, market analysis, and trading strategies. Some of the course content is supplementary to the content of this book and it would be instructive to spend some time surveying what is available.

## BIG CHARTS WEB SITE

This site provides two easily accessed types of charts. One is called, "Quick Charts" and the other is "Interactive Charting." The Quick Chart service gives you a 1-year display of the stock prices and trading volume. No moving averages are shown or available. With the chart is a summary of the day's trading in the stock up to the current time.

The Interactive Charting option allows you to select the time span of the chart from 1 day to 10 years. You can also select a particular year or any other period in the past. And you can compare the price performance of the stock to the market averages or to a variety of other stock indexes.

## QUANTUM ON LINE WEB SITE

This Web site provides extensive information on preferred stocks. For each preferred stock, it shows price of the stock at the initial public offering, the amount of the dividend and whether it is cumulative, and the percentage yield to the investor. It provides the call and maturity dates and the amount to be paid to the investor on the call date. It gives the ratings by Moody's and Standard & Poor's to lets the investor know the investment quality of the issue. It has a link to the stock exchange for a current price quote, volume of trading, the high and low prices during trading, and other data.

To help the investor in the selection of an investment, the site provides a list of all preferred stocks, basic information about preferred stocks, tips on how to invest for income, an explanation of credit ratings, and a glossary of investment terms. If you decide to invest in and/or trade preferred stocks, this is an excellent starting point.

## NATIONAL ASSOCIATION OF REAL ESTATE INVESTMENT TRUSTS (REITs) WEB SITE

This is the prime source of information on REITs on the Internet. It lists all of the publicly traded REITs by name and ticker symbol. Also listed are the names and ticker symbols of all REIT open-ended mutual funds and closed-end funds. A detailed description of the types of real estate in each REIT fund is revealed with a click on its ticker symbol.

The many different types of REITs are described so the investor can select the type that appeals to him or her. For example, some REITs invest in only one type of property such as shopping centers, apartment buildings, warehouses, office buildings, health care facilities, or hotels. Other REITs invest is several of these types of REITs in order to be diversified. Another way REITs diversify is to invest on a nationwide basis, while some REITs only invest in one region of the country or in one metropolitan area. This information is important to a potential REIT investor, and if you want to invest in REITs this site is the place to start your investigation.

# D

# BIBLIOGRAPHY

Darst, David M., *The Art of Asset Allocation*, New York: McGraw-Hill, 2003.

Edwards, Robert D., *Technical Analysis of Stock Trends*, 8th ed., New York: St. Lucie Press, 2001.

Jiler, William L., *How Charts Can Help You in the Stock Market*, New York: Trendline Publishing, 1962.

Meyer, Thomas A., *The Technical Analysis Course*, 3d ed., New York: McGraw-Hill, 2002.

Murphy, John J., *Technical Analysis of Financial Markets*, New York: Prentice Hall Publishing, 1999.

O'Neill, William J., *How to Make Money in Stocks*, New York: McGraw-Hill, 1988.

Pistolese, Clifford A., *Using Technical Analysis*, New York: McGraw-Hill, 1994.

Pring, Martin J., *How To Select Stocks Using Technical Analysis*, New York: McGraw-Hill, 2002.

Rockefeller, Barbara, *Technical Analysis for Dummies*, Hoboken, New Jersey: Wiley Publishing, 2004.

Weiss, Jeffrey, *Beat The Market*, New York: Cloverdale Press, 1985.

Woods, Steve, *Float Analysis*, New York: Wiley Publishing, 2002.

# INDEX